# BREAKFAST AT TIFFANY'S

BY
## TRUMAN CAPOTE

STAGE ADAPTATION BY
## RICHARD GREENBERG

★

★

DRAMATISTS
PLAY SERVICE
INC.

2

BREAKFAST AT TIFFANY'S was originally produced on Broadway by Colin Ingram & Donovan Mannato, Geoffrey Thomas, and Dominic Ianno, at the Cort Theatre, opening on March 20, 2013. It was directed by Sean Mathias, the scenic design was by Derek McLane, the costume design was by Colleen Atwood, the lighting design was by Peter Kaczorowski, the projection design was by Wendall K. Harrington, and the sound design was by Rob Milburn and Michael Bodeen. The cast was as follows:

| | |
|---|---|
| HOLLY GOLIGHTLY | Emilia Clarke |
| FRED | Cory Michael Smith |
| JOE BELL | George Wendt |
| MADAME SPANELLA/LADY BOSS | Suzanne Bertish |
| REPORTER | Danny Binstock |
| JOSE/JOSE'S COUSIN | Pedro Carmo |
| JOURNALIST/COP | Elisabeth Anthony Gray |
| COLONEL/DOC | Murphy Guyer |
| DEPT. STORE OWNER/ DR. GOLDMAN/O.J.'S SERVANT | Eddie Korbich |
| RUSTY'S SERVANT | Paolo Montalban |
| MAG WILDWOOD | Kate Cullen Roberts |
| SID ARBUCK/EDITOR | John Rothman |
| RUSTY TRAWLER | Tony Torn |
| O.J. BERMAN | Lee Wilkof |
| I.Y. YUNIOSHI | James Yaegashi |

# CHARACTERS

FRED

HOLLY GOLIGHTLY

JOE BELL

MADAME SPANELLA

I.Y. YUNIOSHI

RUSTY TRAWLER

O.J. BERMAN

MAG WILDWOOD

DOC

JOSE YBARRA-JAEGAR

EDITOR

### *Ensemble*

SID ARBUCK, AIR FORCE COLONEL, JOURNALIST, MAN, STERN LADY BOSS, DR. GOLDMAN, O.J.'S SERVANT, RUSTY'S SERVANT, REPORTER, FEMALE COP

## ABOUT FRED

When he is speaking directly to us from the play's present tense, a subtle quality is asserted that is withheld otherwise — something insinuating, at ease, even vaguely feline. In the scenes of the past, he's more dedicated to enacting the role of a fine young man.

# BREAKFAST AT TIFFANY'S

## ACT ONE

### Scene 1

*Joe's bar.*

FRED. *(To us.)* In a downpour of October rain, I arrive at a neighborhood of my past, summoned by the ghost of someone who'd never been the least bit spectral. *(Joe Bell enters, fixes a drink, and chews Tums.)* Joe! How are you? *(They shake hands.)*

JOE. Fred! Listen to me — "Fred."

FRED. Fred'll do.

JOE. You're looking richer than you used to.

FRED. And you're still keeping Tums in business, I see.

JOE. Ach, this gut of mine.

FRED. *Plus ça change.*

JOE. What is that supposed to be, French?

FRED. *(Good-humored.)* No. Just pretension.

JOE. Well … Congratulations on … changing, I guess.

FRED. And to you for staying the same. *(They smile. Enough of this awkward talk.)* Well … I've blunderbussed my way through this typhoon to —

JOE. Yeah, yeah — I wouldn't have got you over here if it wasn't a very peculiar thing has happened.

FRED. You heard from Holly.

JOE. Thing is, I don't know.

FRED. Joe.

JOE. That is to say … I want your opinion. You recall a certain Mr. I.Y. Yunioshi. A gentleman from Japan.

FRED. California.

JOE. Don't go mixing me up. But you know who I mean?

FRED. I do. *(To us.)* Our brownstone neighbor. A photographer of some note and the building's most distinguished resident.

JOE. Okay. So last night who comes waltzing in here but this self-same Mr. I.Y. Yunioshi. *(Yunioshi appears in the background, waiting to take his part. He's quite sleek, well-dressed, an artist and a success.)* I haven't seen him, I guess it's over two years. And where do you think he's been these two years?

FRED and YUNIOSHI. *(In unison.)* Africa. *(Joe looks surprised.)*

FRED. I read it in Winchell.

YUNIOSHI. Didn't you read it in Winchell?

JOE. Well, see did you read this in Winchell. *(He extracts photographs from a manila envelope. They appear, rather faintly, elegantly, as projections. They are of a black man in a calico skirt, smiling shyly and displaying a wood carving of a girl's head.)*

FRED. What am I looking at here, Joe?

JOE. Well stop looking at the man in the skirt. Focus on the wood carving.

YUNIOSHI. It is Holly. Unmistakably, Holly Golightly.

JOE. Now what do you make of that?

FRED. Well — it looks like her, sure, but —

JOE. Listen, boy, it *is* her. Sure as I'm a man fit to wear britches. The Jap knew it was her the minute he saw her.

YUNIOSHI. *(At "the minute.")* I knew it the minute I saw her.

FRED. He saw her? In Africa?

JOE and YUNIOSHI. The statue.

JOE. But it comes to the same thing. Read the facts for yourself.

FRED. *(Reverse of photo.)* Wood carving, S Tribe, Tococul, East Anglia, Christmas Day, 1956.

JOE. He was there, the Jap.

YUNIOSHI. In Tococul, a village of mud flats and buzzards on roofs — and of no interest. I'd decided to move on when I saw one fellow — *that* fellow — squatting before his hut with the wood carvings. They were striking. I inspected them, artist to artist. Then I saw this one.

FRED. *(To us.)* Then he saw this one *(And in the photo, the carving is slightly highlighted.)*

YUNIOSHI. I felt like I was falling in a dream.

FRED. He tried to barter.

YUNIOSHI. Ten dollars and a pound of salt! Twenty dollars and a pound of salt!

JOE. He was on to something — Save the statue 'cause that's all you're gonna be *able* to hold on to.

FRED. Finally for a sum of money and a weight of salt, he got not the carving, but its story.

YUNIOSHI. One day three white people came riding out of the bush, two men and a girl. The men, both red-eyed with fever, were forced to stay shut and shivering in an isolated hut, while the young woman, presently having taken a fancy to the wood carver, shared his mat. *(Yunioshi smiles knowingly.)*

JOE. I don't credit that part. I know she had her ways, but I don't think she'd be up to anything as much as that.

YUNIOSHI. She went as she came, rode away on a horse.

JOE. Alone or with the men?

YUNIOSHI. *("Come now.")* Holly Golightly?

JOE. With the two men, I guess.

YUNIOSHI. I asked about her up and down the country. Nobody else had ever seen her. She vanished. Holly Golightly. Gone. *(He exits.)*

FRED. ... Ah. That's all, then.

JOE. One thing you got to admit, it's the only *definite* news in I don't know how many years. All I hope, I hope she's rich. She must be rich. You got to be rich to go mucking around in Africa.

FRED. She's probably never set foot in Africa.

JOE. You know so much, where is she?

FRED. Dead. Or in a crazy-house. Or married. I think she's married and quieted down and maybe right in this city.

JOE. No. I'll tell you why. You take a man like me, a man's been walking in the streets going on ten or twelve years, and all those years he's got his eyes out for one person, and nobody's ever her, don't it stand to reason she's not there? I see pieces of her all the time, a flat little bottom, any skinny girl that walks fast and straight ... *(Beat.)* You think I'm round the bend.

FRED. No. It's just that I didn't know you'd been in love with her. *(Beat.)*

JOE. Drinks on the house.

FRED. I ... It was good to see you, Joe.

JOE. *(Grabs his wrist.)* Hold on. Sure I loved her. But it wasn't that

7

I wanted to touch her. I'm not crazy, I knew how it was. And I swear, it never crossed my mind about Holly. You can love somebody without it being like that. You keep them a stranger, a stranger who's a friend. Do you know what I mean? *(Pause.)*

FRED. *(Painful, somehow.)* Yes.

JOE. Do you believe it? About Africa?

FRED. *(Shrugs.)* ... Anyway, she's gone. *(The rain grows loud, insistent.)*


## Scene 2


*Fred's apartment. Images of rain that clear to reveal a brownstone. As much solid interior as needed, projection of exterior.*


FRED. It was my room, my first, a nonesuch of a space that, in the days when this had been a single-family dwelling, was where they'd domiciled especially despised *femmes de chambre*. It was filled with old furniture of that itchy particular red fabric one associates with long rides on hot trains. The wallpaper was geologic with age and there was a pattern of water damage on the ceiling above my bed that on dissolute evenings I was certain depicted the Shroud of Turin. Needless to say, I adored it. *(Mr. Yunioshi enters.)* You've already met Mr. Yunioshi, soon to be distinguished. Also in residence was Madame Sapphia Spanella. *(Who sails in on roller skates.)* Who roller skated daily in Central Park and was a flattish contralto given to referring to:

MADAME SPANELLA. My days at the Metropolitan Opera.

FRED. Which were spent exclusively in the cheap seats. *(As she skates off.)* She was a fraud and a prig and a troublemaker. There were others whom you won't meet and who don't matter. And there was Holly. Whose hours were different from my sedulous ones, and who for frustrating weeks I knew only as a rather elegantly printed card in a mailbox slot: *(Image of card: Miss Holiday Golightly — traveling.)* Miss Holiday Golightly, Traveling. *(Tastes the phrase.)* Miss Holiday Golightly — Traveling. How I *wondered* ... *(He gets into bed with brandy and a book.)*

# Scene 3

*Fred's apartment and Holly's door. The sound of a door buzzer. Fred listens. Mr. Yunioshi appears. In his robe.*

YUNIOSHI. Miss Golightly, I must protest.

HOLLY. *(Offstage.)* Oh darling, I *am* sorry. I lost the goddamn key.

YUNIOSHI. You cannot go on ringing my bell. You must please, please have yourself a key made.

HOLLY. But I *lose* them *all!*

YUNIOSHI. I work, I have to sleep — but you're always ringing my bell.

HOLLY. Oh *don't* scold me, you *dear* little man. I *won't* do it again. And if you promise not to be angry ... I might let you take those pictures we mentioned.

YUNIOSHI. When? *(Holly appears, trailed by a male nonentity, middle aged. She wears a cocktail dress and dark glasses.)*

HOLLY. Soon.

YUNIOSHI. Any time. *(He retreats. Holly arrives at her level, trailed by the nonentity. Fred spies on her.)*

HOLLY. *(Fussing at her clutch in search of door key.)* Oh dear. *(Finds it.)* Ah-hah! *(To the man who is unavailingly pawing at her.)* Bless you, darling, you were sweet to see me home.

SID ARBUCK. Hey, baby! *(In protest of the door closing in his face.)*

HOLLY. Yes, Harry?

SID ARBUCK. Harry was the other guy. I'm Sid. Sid Arbuck. You like me.

HOLLY. I worship you, Mr. Arbuck. But good night, Mr. Arbuck.

SID ARBUCK. Hey, baby, let me in, baby. You like me, baby, I'm a liked guy. Didn't I pick up the check, five people, *your* friends, I never seen them before?

HOLLY. Mr. Arbuck ...

SID ARBUCK. Yeah?

HOLLY. The next time a girl wants a little powder-room change, take my advice, darling: *Don't* give her twenty cents. *(She slams the door.)*

## Scene 4

*Fred's apartment.*

FRED. She kept her word to Mr. Yunioshi. And took to buzzing my door instead. Midnight. *(Buzz.)* Four, five. *(Buzz, buzz.)* And I, like some mentally defective lab rat in the Pavlov experiment, responded faithfully despite the absence of any evident reward. *(In bed, with brandy and Simenon novel. He feels something, like breath on his neck, intimate menace. Bolts upright.)* What the — *(Holly in bathrobe slips in through his window.)*

HOLLY. Darling, not so loud!

FRED. Um ...

HOLLY. I've got the most terrifying man downstairs. I mean he's sweet when he isn't drunk, but let him start lapping up the vino, and oh God quel beast! If there's one thing I loathe, it's men who bite. *(Loosens robe to show bite marks. She's obviously naked underneath.)* I'm sorry if I frightened you, but that fire escape was damned icy. And you looked so cozy. Like my brother Fred. We used to sleep four in a bed, and he was the only one that ever let me hug him on a cold night. By the way, do you mind if I call you Fred? *(Which is why he's called:)*

FRED. Um —

HOLLY. I suppose you think I'm very brazen or *très fou* or something.

FRED. Not at all. *(She looks disappointed.)*

HOLLY. Yes you do. Everybody does. I don't mind. It's useful. *(She sits in one of his chairs, tucks her legs beneath her, looks around.)* Is this where you live?

FRED. *(Proud?)* Um ... Yes.

HOLLY. How *can* you bear it? It's a chamber of *hor*rors.

FRED. ... Oh, you get used to anything.

HOLLY. I don't. Anybody that does, they might as well be dead. *(Silence.)* It looks as though I'm here for the duration so we ought to converse.

FRED. You're Miss Holiday Golightly.

HOLLY. Only to my creditors.

FRED. I …

HOLLY. I don't mean it. I don't have creditors, I'm cash-only. What I mean is, *you'll* call me Holly.

FRED. And you can call me —

HOLLY. Fred, yes I know, I've already started. On second look, this place wouldn't have to be quite *such* a dungeon if you'd frou-frou it up a bit. Have you given any thought to —

FRED. I think of nothing else.

HOLLY. I'm so glad — What have you come up with?

FRED. *(On the spot.)* … There's a birdcage in that antique store round the corner I'm thinking of —

HOLLY. I don't like things in cages —

FRED. — There's nothing *in* the cage; the cage itself is the attraction — it's all mosques and minarets and bamboo rooms —

HOLLY. *Buy* it, then.

FRED. I'm planning to. It's three hundred and fifty dollars but I expect to make that easily.

HOLLY. Gorgeous.

FRED. Over the next six or seven years.

HOLLY. … Oh. You actually *are* poor, not just playacting. *Quel triste.* Well — you're not the type anyway, pretty though you are. The eyes are the giveaway. What do you do all day so prettily in this … atelier?

FRED. *(It hits him.)* Did you just *break* into my apartment and … I write things.

HOLLY. *Do* you! Maybe you'll write about me. Lots of people have — or mean to; anyway I'd be a marvelous subject.

FRED. No, I don't think so.

HOLLY. Don't be rude.

FRED. No no no — it's just that I only write about the past.

HOLLY. No such place. What do you write about in this "past" of yours?

FRED. Things I've lost. Things that are gone.

HOLLY. That'll be me soon enough. I've never been to bed with a writer.

FRED. … Um … what a thing!

HOLLY. No, wait: do you know Benny Shacklett? *(He doesn't.)* That's funny. He's written an awful lot of radio stuff. But quel rat. Tell me are you a *real* writer?

FRED. Of *course* I — What do you mean?

11

HOLLY. Does anybody *buy* what you write?

FRED. ... Oh. I'm *new*, you know. I'm sending out a group of my stories this week and I expect —

HOLLY. Enclose your photograph.

FRED. Is that done?

HOLLY. In your case, yes. Oh! I'm going to help you. I can, too. Think of all the people I know who know people. I'm going to help you because you look like my brother Fred. Only smaller. I haven't seen him since I was fourteen, that's when I left home, and he was already six-feet-four. It was the peanut butter that made Fred so tall. Everybody thought it was dotty the way he gorged himself on peanut butter. But he wasn't dotty, just sweet and vague and terribly slow; he'd been in the eighth grade three years when I ran away. Poor Fred. I wonder if the army's generous with their peanut butter. Which reminds me, I'm starving. You don't mind. *(She helps herself to an apple from a bowl on his table.)*

FRED. How did you come to leave home so young? *(She bites the apple, scratches her nose. Maybe she hasn't heard him.)* How did you come to leave home so young? *(She examines the apple.)* I ask because it's the age when we'd all *like* to leave home but most of us haven't the gumption ...

HOLLY. *(As though it hadn't happened.)* Tell me something you've written. The story part.

FRED. Oh! Oh ... Oh. Well — They're not the kind of stories you *can* tell.

HOLLY. Too dirty?

FRED. No, it's that — too dirty?! No, I ... Maybe I'll let you read one sometime.

HOLLY. This apple needs a chaser. Fix me a drink, darling. Then you can read me a story yourself.

FRED. *(Fixes drink, hands it to her, talks to us — some chagrin.)* Very few authors, especially the unpublished, can resist the invitation to read aloud. It was a story I'd finished the day before. I remember little about it — count your blessings — but it dealt with two women school teachers who had been touched by the breath of scandal and ... events transpired. It featured phrases like "the scent of strong black coffee in pewter cups" and "the immemorial crackle of burning leaves" and "a sorrow for which no name had yet been devised." *(With each phrase, Holly reacts unfavorably.)* Then it was over. *(Pause. Holly listens for more.)*

HOLLY. Is that the *end*?

FRED. ... Why ... it — why *wouldn't* it be?

HOLLY. Of course I like dykes themselves. They don't scare me a bit. But stories about dykes bore the bejesus out of me. I just can't put myself in their shoes. Incidentally, do you know any nice lesbians? I'm looking for a roommate. Don't laugh; really, they make wonderful homemakers, you never have to worry about brooms and defrosting and sending out the laundry. I had a dyke roommate in Hollywood, we called her the Lone Ranger — of course people couldn't help think I was a dyke myself. And of course I am. Everyone is a bit. So what. *(Pause.)*

FRED. *(In a voice of controlled murder.)* It's not about dykes.

HOLLY. ... Oh? Well, then, what *is* it about? *(He stays silent, she notices his alarm clock.)* That clock *lies*! It's not 4:30, it can't be! Is this Thursday?

FRED. Yes.

HOLLY. How gruesome.

FRED. As anyone who'd been really *listening* could tell it's about what happens when — *(Interested belatedly.)* What's gruesome about Thursday?

HOLLY. Nothing. Except that I can never remember when it's coming. You see, on Thursdays I have to catch the 8:45. I've *got* to stay awake, *(She pinches her cheeks.)* there isn't time to sleep, I'd look consumptive, I'd sag like a tenement, and that wouldn't be fair: A girl can't go to Sing Sing with a green face.

FRED. God no — not with their standards.

HOLLY. Oh look — I'm keeping you awake. Go to sleep.

FRED. No! Please. Why do you go to —

HOLLY. No — I'm not going to tell you about Sally. That wouldn't be cricket. Of course, they never *told* me not to tell anyone. In so many words. Maybe you could put it in a story, with different names and whatnot.

FRED. I told you, I don't write about —

HOLLY. Stop being *dreary*. All right then, out of my devotion to your career: His name is Sally Tomato, and I speak Yiddish better than he speaks English, but he's a darling old man, terribly pious. He'd look like a monk if it weren't for the gold teeth. Anyway, he saw me in Joe Bell's before Sing Sing and just couldn't shake the vision. So he sent his lawyer to get me. Mr. O'Shaughnessy — that's the lawyer — asked me how I'd like to cheer up a lonely old

13

man, at the same time pick up a hundred a week. I told him, look, darling, you've got the wrong Miss Golightly, I'm not a nurse that does tricks on the side. I wasn't impressed by the honorarium, either; you can do as well as that on trips to the powder room: Any gent with the slightest chic will give you fifty for the girl's john, and I always ask for cab fare too, that's another fifty. But then he told me his client was Sally Tomato. He said dear old Sally had always admired me *à la distance*, so wouldn't it be a good deed if I went to visit him once a week. Well, I couldn't say no: it was too romantic.

FRED. And all you do is … converse?

HOLLY. Practically.

FRED. *(This doesn't sound right.)* They don't let just *anyone* visit prisoners —

HOLLY. Of *course* they don't, darling. I say I'm his niece. It's all on the up-and-up. Listen: I leave the weather report and Mr. O'Shaughnessy mails me the hundred in cash.

FRED. What's the weather report?

HOLLY. Just messages I leave with the answering service so Mr. O'Shaughnessy will know for sure that I've been there. Sally tells me what to say, things like, oh, "There's a hurricane in Cuba" and "It's snowing in Palermo."

FRED. … Um —

HOLLY. Don't worry, darling, it's all perfectly kosher. I've been taking care of myself a long time. Oh — I'm all in — ! *(She lies beside him in the bed.)* Do you mind? I only want to rest a moment. So let's don't say another word. Go to sleep. *(She drifts off, curled into his body.)*

FRED. *(To us.)* It was for nights like this that I'd come to New York. *(He contemplates her, amazed. Light changes with them like this, time passing. She puts her hand on his arm, still asleep.)*

HOLLY. Poor Fred. Where are you, Fred? Because it's cold. There's snow in the wind. *(Her cheek is on his shoulder. Tears.)*

FRED. Why are you crying?

HOLLY. *(Springs up.)* Oh, for God's sake — I *hate* snoops! *(She's out the window and away.)*

FRED. *(At her wake.)* Holly? — ! *(He looks at us, perplexed. Lights. As he puts on jacket and tie, Holly appears outside his door, dumps a gift basket. Fred goes to it, removes card, reads.)*

HOLLY. *(Out.)* Bless you, darling Fred. Please forgive the other night. You were an angel about the whole thing. *Mille tendresse —* Holly. P.S. I won't bother you again. *(He turns the card over, writes*

*on it.)*
FRED.  Please do. *(Deposits it at her door.)* And she vanished from my life. *(He smiles self-mockingly.)*


## Scene 5


*Projections give us/say "21 Club" ... Fred joins Editor — middle-aged, bluff — at table.*


EDITOR.  Very impressed, very impressive. Your stories. Why aren't you drinking more?
FRED.  I don't drink much.
EDITOR.  I gotta get my licks in in town. Back in Darien, the wife has me on a three-drink limit. Can you imagine? Wife, three daughters; I'm surrounded. You know that female *fume*?
FRED.  *(Noncommittal but fetching smile.)* I ... no.
EDITOR.  *(Darkly.)* Well, you will. *(New topic.)* Your *prose* though, that orchidaceous Southern —
FRED.  Thank you very much.
EDITOR.  "A sorrow for which no name had yet been devised." Haunting.
FRED.  I'm so glad.
EDITOR.  Course at the houses, we're all playing a waiting game. It's all about who comes back from the war and gets to be the next Stephen Crane — I don't suppose we can expect a war novel from *you* —
FRED.  ... I'm more concerned with the interiors of things, the spiritual —
EDITOR.  Loved the photo, by the way.
FRED.  Thank you.
EDITOR.  Provocative pose. Unique. The photographer...?
FRED.  Someone I met and ... did a favor for and in return he ...
EDITOR.  You married?
FRED.  No.
EDITOR.  Girlfriend?
FRED.  ... Not at the moment.
EDITOR.  Pretty girlfriend's a good thing for an author to have.

They go over well at parties.

FRED. I see. Well, there are girls I'm *int*erested in, of —

EDITOR. I expect we'll be seeing you at a *lot* of parties.

FRED. Well … I … *hope* so. (*Editor puts his hand over Fred's in a jovial, paternal way. Lets it linger there. Fred allows it. Something a little hard and whorish comes into his eyes. Editor senses the change.*)

EDITOR. Let's shake on that. (*Turns the hold into a shake. Holly at the entrance in her nighttime regalia, dark glasses and flanking men. They sit at the next table.*)

FRED. My God.

EDITOR. (*Rises.*) I gotta go to the john. (*Fred looks at him.*) John's in *that* direction. 'Case you have an urgent need. (*He goes.*)

HOLLY. My, my.

FRED. My indeed.

HOLLY. Ye-e-es.

FRED. Funny we meet here.

HOLLY. Isn't it?

FRED. What with us living only a few vertical yards apart and never seeing each other at all. I've lamented your absence.

HOLLY. Darling: "Lamented"? *Have* you?

FRED. Where've you been?

HOLLY. Out and about. *You're* certainly keeping distingue company.

FRED. Oh. Do you recognize him?

HOLLY. *Mon ange*, I'm not moss, I mean, I don't live under a rock.

FRED. I sent him a couple of stories and —

HOLLY. Did you enclose your photo like I —

FRED. I was told that was standard practice —

HOLLY. Whatever works, darling; don't blush.

FRED. Anyway, he quite liked them; the *stories*, that —

HOLLY. As who wouldn't? I haven't been able to get that one you read me out of my mind; it *rattles* me.

FRED. You were bored silly.

HOLLY. Delayed re*a*ction, darling. I'm positively *trailed* by it. "A sorrow for which no name had yet been devised." *La conditione humaine.*

FRED. I'm — yes. (*Beat.*) And who are *your* friends?

HOLLY. That's the awful thing; I haven't got any. I'm unutterably alone.

FRED. The gentlemen at the table … I mean?

HOLLY. Oh these! *Quel hilarité!* I forgot they were there. Mr. Luce,

Mr. Rockefeller — Fred. *(They murmur something in lockjaw.)*
FRED. You're keeping rather swank company, yourself.
HOLLY. It's always the same — Old Money and sour breath. These *even*ings.
FRED. Isn't it strange?
HOLLY. So very.
FRED. All of it.
HOLLY. Yes.
FRED. Do you think it means something that we've run into each other, here in this ... citadel?
HOLLY. Do you?
FRED. I might. If I were still young and credulous enough to believe in Fate.
HOLLY. You have such pretty eyes.
FRED. Holly ... *(And even in this fantasy, he can't conjure the next thing to say.)*
HOLLY. Say Fred, what say we ditch these plutocrats and hie ourselves to Longchamps and eat chess pie and swill bootleg hootch then stumble through the streets in an ecstasy of alcohol and get run over by a couple of taxicabs and stagger home in the wee small hours of some far-flung morning and fall into bed like that night, that magical night, and tell each other our very most secret lies? Wouldn't you like that? Wouldn't it *save* us? *(And a subtle light shift.)*
FRED. Except she didn't see me. Those dark glasses had concrete panes. Or maybe she was blinded by boredom. Either way. *(Holly and the men leave.)*

## Scene 6

*Projection: Cityscape. Fred walks. At last, he's sadly home.*

FRED. Holly became a chronic absence and because I was still new to the city and so alone, I took that personally. I was the very *subject* of her indifference, its epicenter and cause. I tried changing my hours to conform to hers. No dice. I found myself rooting through the trash basket outside her door. *(Images accompany:)* There were tabloids and travel folders and astrological charts. And V-letters by the bale-full, torn into strips like bookmarks, though I read them like books. These were the words that recurred: *Remember* and *miss you* and *rain* and *please write* and *damn* and *goddamn* and *lonesome* and *love*. And angling my body so as not to be seen, I one day saw this:

## Scene 7

> *Holly appears on her fire escape, strumming a guitar. Fred watches from his apartment. She sings a hillbilly ballad. Very lonely, and simple, and piercing.*

HOLLY.
> *I am a traveling creature*
> *a-traveling through this land*
> *Today I am a warning*
> *to woman and to man.*
> *Mother hold my hand,*
> *hold up my dyin' day.*
>
> *I met a simple woman*
> *in a far-off distant land.*
> *She came to me a-weeping,*
> *she gave to me her hand.*
> *Mother hold my hand,*
> *hold up my dyin' day.*
>
> *I asked that simple woman*
> *if she ever tried to pray.*
> *She said I did this morning*
> *but the spirit did delay.*
> *Mother hold my hand*
> *hold up my dyin' day.*
> *(She disappears inside.)*

## Scene 8

*Fred's apartment. Fred alone for a moment and staggered. A sudden inspiration and he scrawls something on a piece of paper, and leaves his apartment. Madame Spanella appears.*

## Scene 9

MADAME SPANELLA. You are a nice young man! Save yourself from her!
FRED. Oh! *Skate* somewhere, will you?
MADAME SPANELLA. I am not wearing skates! I do not skate when I am saving lives!
FRED. *(Reads what he's written.)* "Just a reminder. Tomorrow is Thursday. Your neighbor, Fred." *(He slips it under her door. Holly, in a towel, slips an answering note under his.)*
HOLLY. "Bless you for reminding me. Can you stop for a drink tonight 6ish?"
FRED. Yes! I *can*! *(Holly back to her apartment, then disappears.)*

## Scene 10

*Holly's apartment. Fred straightens his tie, knocks on her door. The door opens. O.J. Berman, a Hollywood elf, answers.*

O.J. How do?
FRED. Hello?
O.J. Kid's in the shower. You expected?
FRED. I — oh, then there are to be *others*? ... Yes I am expected.
O.J. A lot of characters come here, they're not expected. You know

the kid long?

FRED.  Not very.

O.J.  So you don't know the kid long?

FRED.  I live upstairs.

O.J.  You got the same layout?

FRED.  Much smaller. Is this, then to be a —

O.J.  *(Taps ash onto floor.)* This is a dump. This is unbelievable. But the kid don't know how to live even when she's got the dough. So, what do you think: Is she or ain't she?

FRED.  Ain't she what?

O.J.  A phony.

FRED.  I wouldn't have thought so.

O.J.  You're wrong. She is a phony. But on the other hand you're right. She isn't a phony because she's a *real* phony. She believes all this crap she believes. You can't talk her out of it. I've tried with tears running down my cheeks. Benny Polan, respected everywhere, Benny Polan tried. Benny had it on his mind to marry her, she don't go for it, Benny spent maybe thousands sending her to head-shrinkers. Even the famous one, the one can only speak German, boy, did he throw in the towel. Mind you, I like the kid. Everybody does, but there's lots that don't. But I'll tell you the truth. You can beat your brains out for her, and she'll hand you horseshit on a platter. To give an example — who is she like you see her today? She's strictly a girl you'll read where she ends up at the bottom of a bottle of Seconals. I've seen it happen more times than you got toes, and those kids, they weren't even nuts. *She's* nuts.

FRED.  But —

O.J.  Now a couple of years back, out on the Coast, there was a time when it could've been different. I know, see, 'cause I'm the guy was giving her the push. O.J. Berman. *(Fred lifts his eyebrows, impressed.)* I'm the first one who saw her. Out at Santa Anita. She's stylish: She's okay; she comes across. Even when she's wearing glasses *this* thick, even when she opens her mouth and you don't know if she's an Okie or a hillbilly or what. I still don't. My guess, nobody'll ever know where she came from. She's such a goddamn liar, maybe she don't know herself anymore. But it took us a year to smooth out that accent. How we did it finally, we gave her French lessons: After she could imitate French it wasn't so long she could imitate English. So now she sounds English-like, like Hollywood, like everybody, it's good. People were interested, big ones, and to top it all, Benny

Polan, a respected guy, Benny wants to marry her. An agent could ask for more? Then wham! *The Story of Dr. Wassell.* You see that picture? Cecil B. DeMille. Gary Cooper. Jesus, I kill myself; it's all set: They're going to test her for the part of Dr. Wassell's nurse. One of his nurses anyway. Then wham! The phone rings. She says, "This is Holly," I say, "Honey you sound far away," she says "I'm in New York," I say "What the hell are you doing in New York when it's Sunday and you got the test tomorrow?" She says "I'm in New York 'cause I've never been to New York." I say "Get your ass on a plane and get back here," she says "I don't want it." I say, "What's your angle, doll?" She says "You got to want it to be good and I don't want it." I say, "Well what the hell do you want," and she says "When I find out you'll be the first to know." See what I mean: horseshit on a platter. *This* is what she wants? A lot of characters that aren't expected? Living off tips. Running around with bums. So maybe she could marry Rusty Trawler? You should pin a medal on her for that?

FRED. Who is that? Rusty Trawler.

O.J. You don't know Rusty Trawler, you can't know much about the kid. Bad deal. I was hoping you maybe had influence. Could level with the kid before it's too late.

FRED. You said it already is.

O.J. *(Blows smoke ring, smiles gently.)* I could get it rolling again. Like I told you. I sincerely like the kid. *(Holly enters, still in towel.)*

HOLLY. Good, you've met! O.J., Fred is a pure genius-rated writer. Fred, talk to O.J., he can do you a power of good. You two make a contract and if anyone rings, let them in. *(She's off.)*

FRED. So — there are to be others?

O.J. What? You thought it was just you, me, and her? I don't go that way. And neither does the kid, last I heard —

FRED. So it's a *party.*

O.J. I think a small gathering.

FRED. *(To us.)* Enter: the population of Manhattan. *(Both real and shadow people start to crowd the room and fill it with a hum both live and recorded.)* It was one of those louche New York parties that I would come to know so well, the best kind where the guests might equally have arrived by taxi or Black Maria. *(As they enter or flicker in.)* Madame Spanella entered a brief protest.

MADAME SPANELLA. I will call the Housing Board! I will call the gendarmes! I must practice my scales! *(She's elbowed out, emitting hysterical arpeggios.)*

FRED. As yet unused to this caliber of noise, I found myself gravitating toward a place of relative spaciousness: Holly's bookshelf. On which I found exactly one volume. *The Baseball Guide*, curiously. From inside *The Baseball Guide* fell a veritable scrapbook of clippings, devoted chiefly to the aforementioned Rusty Trawler. *(Rusty Trawler, an unborn-looking nonesuch, cannonballs in.)*

RUSTY. Now the party's starting!

FRED. Incredibly, *this* was Rusty Trawler. This ... anthropoid, this pickled infant —

HOLLY. Rusty, help the captain with a refill, would you? *(The party people, real and projected, move and Rusty moves among them.)*

RUSTY. Yup, darling, yup, anything for you, yup.

FRED. *(Brandishing clippings.)* According to my research, he'd been a tabloid sensation: Orphaned by five. Father killed by an anarchist, mother died of shock. Guardian fiddled scandalously with his privates. Married four times, divorced four times; his last wife incited a mutiny on his yacht that left him stranded on the Dry Tortugas, making her my favorite among his wives.

RUSTY. *(Bubbling through the party.)* You know what *really* stinks about this war? You can't get a goddamn taxicab HRYACK!

HOLLY. Rusty, this gentleman's cup is dry —

FRED. Winchell repeatedly referred to him as a Nazi chiefly because he was ... um ... a Nazi. I would find out the cab it had been so hard for him to obtain had borne him from a meeting in the environs of 92nd Street. *Heil! (Holly joins him.)*

HOLLY. Admiring my publicity or are you just a baseball fan?

FRED. What was this week's weather report?

HOLLY. Nix on that darling. I *loathe* baseball but it's part of my research. There're so few things men can talk about. And how are you making out with O.J.?

FRED. We've separated by mutual agreement.

HOLLY. He can *help* you.

FRED. A sequel to *Dr. Wassell's* in the works, is it?

HOLLY. Oh. He's still harping? Well, he's got a point. I *should* feel guilty. I let him go on dreaming when I wasn't dreaming a bit. I was just vamping for time to make a few self-improvements. I know damn well I'd never be a movie star; my complexes aren't inferior enough. I don't mean I'd mind being rich and famous, but if it happens, I'd like to have my ego tagging along. I want to still be me when I wake up one fine morning and have breakfast at Tiffany's. You need a glass. Rusty!

22

RUSTY. *(Waddles over with the cat.)* Yuh, darling?

HOLLY. Will you bring my friend a drink.

FRED. Scotch neat.

RUSTY. *(Hands her the cat.)* Yup. Take him. It's hard to stir.

HOLLY. *(Stroking cat.)* Poor slob. Poor slob without a name. It's a little inconvenient, his not having a name. But I haven't any right to give him one: He'll have to wait until he *belongs* to somebody.

FRED. How'd he come to be your roommate, anyway? He doesn't look like a lesbian.

HOLLY. We just sort of took up by the river one day: He's an independent, and so am I.

FRED. Doesn't take much to own a cat; just feed him and he's yours.

HOLLY. No — I don't want to own anything until I know I've found the place where me and things belong together. I don't know where that is just yet. But I know what it's like.

FRED. Tell me.

HOLLY. It's like Tiffany's.

FRED. The breakfast joint?

HOLLY. Yes. There. You know those days when you've got the mean reds?

FRED. Are they the same as the blues?

HOLLY. No ... *No.* The blues are because you're getting fat or maybe it's been raining too long. You're sad, that's all. But the mean reds are horrible. You're afraid and you sweat like hell, but you don't know what you're afraid of. Except something bad is going to happen, only you don't know what it is. You've had that feeling.

FRED. So often.

HOLLY. What I've found does the most good is just to get into a taxi and go to Tiffany's. It calms me down right away, the quietness and the proud look of it. Nothing very bad could happen to you there, not with those kind men in their nice suits, and that lovely smell of silver and alligator wallets. If I could find a real-life place that made me feel like Tiffany's, then I'd buy some furniture and give the cat a name. I've thought maybe after the war, Fred and I ... I went to Mexico once. It's a wonderful country for raising horses. I saw one place near the sea. Fred's good with horses. *(She goes dreamy. He touches her face. Holds her. She lets him. They're thinking of different things.)*

RUSTY. What's *this*?

HOLLY. Don't be an idiot. It's nothing.

RUSTY. ... *Tell* me about it.

HOLLY. *(Admonishing.)* Rusty.

RUSTY. *(Mild disappointment.)* Oh well. I'm hungry. It's seven-thirty and I'm hungry. You know what the doctor said.

HOLLY. Yes, Rusty. I know what the doctor said.

RUSTY. Well, then let's *go.*

HOLLY. I want you to behave, Rusty.

RUSTY. You don't love me.

HOLLY. Nobody loves naughtiness.

RUSTY. *(Excited by that.) Do* you love me?

HOLLY. *(Pats him.)* Tend to your chores, Rusty. And when I'm ready, we'll go eat wherever you want.

RUSTY. Chinatown?

HOLLY. But that doesn't mean sweet and sour spareribs. You know what the doctor said. *(She hands him the cat.)*

RUSTY. *(Satisfied.)* All right. *(Waddles off.)* All right.

FRED. You *don't* love him, do you? You couldn't.

HOLLY. You can make yourself love anybody. *(Just then, a voice like a gong.)*

MAG. H-h-holly Go*light*ly!

HOLLY. Oh *crap*!

FRED. What's that?

HOLLY. This boring girl who shows up places and tries to steal people from you; it's pathetic really. I try to be kind to her. *(The answer: Mag Wildwood, all striking ectomorphic 6-plus feet of her.)*

MAG. H-h-holly, you miserable h-h-hoarder! Hogging all these simply r-r-riveting m-m-men! *(The party people incline toward her.)*

HOLLY. Were you invited?

MAG. W-w-was anyb-body? *(She tosses her head back in laughter; so do the party people.)* I've been upstairs working with Yunioshi. Christmas stuff for the *Ba-bazaar.* But you sound vexed, sugar. You b-b-boys not vexed at me for b-b-butting in on your party?

RUSTY. *(Titters, squeezes her.)* Could you use a drink?

MAG. I surely could. Make mine bourbon.

HOLLY. There isn't any.

AIR FORCE COLONEL. I'll gladly run out for some.

MAG. Oh, I declare, let's not have a f-f-fuss. I'm happy with ammonia. Holly honey, don't you bother about me, I can introduce myself. *(To O.J.)* I'm Mag W-w-wildwood from Wildw-w-wood, Arkansas — that's hill country.

FRED. And suddenly, Mag Wildwood from Wildwood, Arkansas,

galvanized the room. *(The speeches tumbling:)*

O.J. O.J. Berman. Pleased to meet you. Maybe you've heard of me? If not, you must've seen some of my pictures. *How Green Were Our Grapes? The Sacred Fount? Milton's Millions? / Mr. Wrigley Buys a Town?*

RUSTY. Lemme get you that drink, honey. Drink's on me. 'Course you could be on me too, if you'd like HRYACK! / No bourbon? Whaddya say to scotch? Gin? Absinthe? Turpentine? HRYACK!

MAN. I believe I saw your layout in last month's *Vogue*. In charmeuse, was it? You, was it? / I *ask* because I own several department stores therefore …

JOURNALIST. We saw each other at the Tazwells. You expressed some interest in meeting Adela Rogers St. Johns. Well …

FRED. *(To us.)* And as this spectacle unfolded, Holly … bided. *(To Holly.)* Is everything all right?

HOLLY. *(Mid-calculation.)* Couldn't be better, darling.

MAG. Who can tell me wh-wh-where is the john?

O.J. Let me take you there.

HOLLY. That won't be necessary. She knows where it is. She's been here before.

MAG. … My yes. I *have*! This p-p-positive h-haze of men — I've gone g-giddy. *(Exits to bathroom.)*

FRED. *(To us.)* And Holly struck. *(Once Mag's gone:)*

HOLLY. It's really very sad. *(Some turn to her; she waits for a few more.)* And so mysterious. You'd think it would *show* more. But heaven knows, she *looks* healthy. So well *clean*. That's the extraordinary part. Wouldn't you — *(To no one in particular.)* I say, wouldn't you say she *looked* clean? *(Someone coughs. A few projections turn their back.)* But I hear so many of these Southern girls have the same trouble. *(Mag returns; a turning from her happens.)*

MAG. Now who has m-m-my *bev*erage? *(Someone real or shadow turns away.)*

FRED. You're diabolical!

HOLLY. I like you, too.

MAG. D-don't you just l-love p-parties like this where everyone is so a-attractive? Hey baby! *(Slight shifting, a solo cough.)*

FRED. The party — Holly-poisoned — dispersed with startling speed while Mag — poor, puzzled Mag — spat invective at it.

MAG. *(To someone leaving.)* Yeah, w-well y-you couldn't get it up with a c-crane anyway. *(As O.J. passes.)* Your movies stink. *(Staring down at Rusty.)* You know what's going to happen to you? I'm going to march you over to the zoo and feed you to the yak.

RUSTY. *(Delighted.)* When? *(Holly gives him a commanding look.)*

MAG. Y-you — you're behind this, H-holly Golightly! H-holly as in "H-hollywood whore" — that's who y-you are! *(She falls to the floor.)*

HOLLY. You're a bore. Get up from there. *(To the last of the party clustering at her door.)* I'll be right there! Be an angel, would you, Fred? Put her in a taxi. She lives at the Winslow.

FRED. Uh sure, but —

MAG. Don't. Live Barbizon. Regent 4-5700. Ask for Mag Wildwood.

HOLLY. You *are* an angel, Fred.

FRED. But where will you *be*? Where shall I *meet* you? *(Holly and the remnant scatter. Fred is left alone with prostrate Mag. She rises on her own steam.)*

MAG. Let's go, stork. Catch lucky balloon. *(She falls flat on her face again. Fred regards her.)*

FRED. Shit. *(He kneels down to attend.)* Hey…? Hey…? *(Tries to wake her, no dice. Takes her pulse, rises.)* You'll be fine. *(He grabs a bottle of scotch.)* So will I. My 100-proof companion saw me fitfully into a sleepy morning. And the next morning. And the one after.


## Scene 11


*Jose enters. Crisp, handsome, in a perfectly tailored suit. He knocks on Fred's door. [When Jose speaks, it is in a charmingly impenetrable accent.]*


FRED. Oh, damn. *(Trudges to door.)* Who is that? *(Opens door a crack.)*

JOSE. Is this the apartment of…?

FRED. Pardon? *(Can't help taking in the gorgeousness that is Jose.)* Oh, hello. *(Butching up.)* Hello.

JOSE. *(Charming.)* I wonder do I have the address correctly?

FRED. The … address?

JOSE. Correctness? Have I it?

FRED. I can't say for *sure* but I suspect: no.

JOSE. I am so pleased to be meeting with you. I am Jose Ybarra-Jaegar. And may I have the pleasure of you? *(He extends his hand.)*

FRED. I am ... just call me Fred.

JOSE. You are Fred.

FRED. As much as I'm anyone these days.

JOSE. Pardon. My English.

FRED. Even in English it's a puzzlement. I don't know why you're here —

JOSE. I and my luggage are come to the apartment of ...

FRED. Umm...?

JOSE. I am so sorry, let me reminisce myself a moment; I lost the paper upon which I wrote the name — Festival Golightly!

FRED. Oh *really*? Holly? You're here to see —

JOSE. ... Who is habitating Mag. Signora Wildwood.

FRED. Ooooooh ... ye-e-es. You've overshot the mark, I'm afraid.

JOSE. *(Alarmed.)* I am contrite!

FRED. N-non-no ... down one floor.

JOSE. Yes.

FRED. Here ... I'll *(And he accompanies him to Holly's.)* The door is doubtless unlocked. *(Jose, politely, opens door. Holly enters from outside.)*

HOLLY. *(To Fred.)* You! *(Notes Jose.)* Oh.

FRED. Oh! Um, Holly, this is Jose ... Something-something.

JOSE. *(Smiles, nods.)* Hello.

HOLLY. Hello. *(Jose disappears into Holly's apartment. Dry:)* That's interesting. *(To Fred.)* Listen, buster, you're not off the hook with me about the other night. I got home and there was Mag on the verge of pneumonia with a hangover out to here and the mean reds on top of it. You were meant to evict her, cher rat, not just leave her here.

FRED. I'm sorry. Abandonment was the theme of the evening so it seemed —

HOLLY. What's that?

FRED. I'm merely saying that *I*, too ... was abandoned.

HOLLY. Oh darling, how dreadful! By whom? *(Beat.)*

FRED. Why didn't you kick her out once she sobered up?

HOLLY. How could I? She's my dearest friend in the whole world. *(She enters apartment. Image of revised mailbox card: Miss Holiday Golightly and Miss Mag Wildwood — traveling together.)*

## Scene 12

*Mag and Holly sun themselves on Holly's fire escape. Fred secretively watching.*

MAG. If you ask me, I think you're l-l-lucky. At least there's one thing you can say for Rusty. He's an American.

HOLLY. Bully for him.

MAG. *Sugar.* There's a war on.

HOLLY. And when it's over, you've seen the last of me, boy.

MAG. I don't feel that way, I'm pr-p-proud of my country. The men in my family were great soldiers. There's a statue of Papadaddy Wildwood smack in the middle of Wildwood. If only I could get used to the idea of m-m-marrying a Brazilian. And *being* a B-brazilian myself. It's such a canyon to cross. Six thousand miles, and not knowing the language —

HOLLY. Go to Berlitz.

MAG. Why on earth would they be teaching P-p-portuguese? It isn't as though anyone spoke it. No, my only chance is to try and make Jose forget politics and become an American. It's such a useless thing for a man to want to be: the p-p-president of *Brazil*. I must be madly in love. You saw us together. Do you think I'm madly in love?

HOLLY. Hard to say — How does he look naked?

MAG. Holly! I'm a very-very-very *conventional* person.

HOLLY. Oh, balls. If you don't even want to *look* at him, I'd say he's getting a pretty cold plate of macaroni. You can't possibly be in love with him.

MAG. I am a warm-hearted person. It's the basis of my character. Do you realize I've knitted ten pairs of argyles in less than three months? And this is the second sweater. Sweaters in Brazil! I ought to be making sun helmets.

HOLLY. It must be winter sometimes.

MAG. ... I know it rains. Rain. Heat. J-j-jungles.

HOLLY. Heat and jungles ... I'd like that.

MAG. Better you than me.

HOLLY. Yes ... Better me than you.

# Scene 13

FRED. *(To us.)* Better her than her. And so they were a foursome. Occasionally, I made it a fivesome but mostly when I wasn't at work — Oh, right: I got a job. The coffers finally empty, I found myself toiling as a slavey in a magazine that was lousy with prestige, *(Projection: Eustace Tilley.)* and to those of us who worked there, just plain ... well. In the rare hours when I wasn't at the office assassinating my youth, I immured myself in my quarters and wrote. They danced. *(Mag and Rusty and Jose and Holly, dancing. Fred anchored in his room, watching and on occasion speaking.)*

RUSTY. *(To Mag.)* You're quite a drink of water.

MAG. And you are some kind of a man.

JOSE. Is this, would you say, a typical gathering of Americans?

HOLLY. Yes, darling, this is exactly how Americans are. In seaport towns and way up in the mountains, and in the hardscrabble South everyone dances, dances, dances. It's the national character.

JOSE. Thank you for the information.

RUSTY. What's your opinion of Mussolini?

MAG. W-well, I'm just a simple girl from Arkansas and don't know a *th-thing* about politics but I will say this: The fascists have a lot more *style* than the D-democrats. You *f-find* that overseas.

RUSTY. You're a vixen!

MAG. Br-brown is the new bl-black!

RUSTY. Uh-huh.

MAG. Though pink is the navy blue of In-india.

JOSE. Your accent — it is different from Mag, is it not?

HOLLY. Yes, darling, worlds apart.

JOSE. I study this — I have Mag help me to learn the English of the people.

HOLLY. I simply adore Mag and would never let *another* person say a word against her, but: Don't do that.

JOSE. Then perhaps you will help? I can study under you.

HOLLY. And you will help me with my Portuguese.

JOSE. Is that of interest?

HOLLY. Oh — I *adore* Brazil. It's always been my *dream* to live there someday.

JOSE. Very good. We will make the exchange. *(They switch partners.)* I am having a marvelous time.

FRED. Your English, Jose.

JOSE. Yes.

FRED. It's improving.

JOSE. Oh yes. It had to. Before: quel rotten! Now I have fine tutors.

FRED. That's impressive.

JOSE. Well, I must learn. If I am to be a diplomat and then … who knows?

FRED. The president of Brazil.

JOSE. *(Modestly.)* Who knows? This is the American Century. How fortunate I am to have found myself in the company of such representative American types. *(Perhaps a slight rise of lights on the patrons, real and shadow, of this club, the posh freak show.)*

FRED. *(Reads; writes.)* While they danced, I kept a journal; it was excruciating. *(Reads; writes.)* Time continues to pass without meaning. My days are rivered with anxiety, failure, poverty, hunger; almost Russian in their dark, soul-scuppering hopelessness. *(He rolls his eyes.)* There was a disturbing episode in the supply room at work this week. I found Q waiting there; apparently he thought I — *(Thinks better of this. To us.)* You don't need to hear this. Holly. How I wish I could write about her! But I'm still comfortable only with what's over and settled and there's a quality about her that suggests she will never belong to the past. She shimmers with events, with the promise of next things. God knows that's what I need: For something at long last to happen. *(Out.)* And It did. *(He picks up an envelope, opens it, reads. Races to Holly's.)* Holly! Holly!

## Scene 14

*Holly opens her door.*

HOLLY. My God, such a racket! What gives?

FRED. My story is being published!

HOLLY. *(Hugs.)* Oh Fred, how marvelous! Dinner at 21 paid off, did it?

FRED. ... What?

HOLLY. Well, you *didn't* think I mistook that scene for the raptures of first love.

FRED. I thought — you didn't *see* me —

HOLLY. Discretion at work, darling — I'm told when the old married ones latch on to a pretty boy, they're so damn grateful you just want to say, "Oh shut up and stick it somewhere, will you?"

FRED. *(Rigid.)* I don't know what you're talking about.

HOLLY. ... All right.

FRED. Anyway, this is a dif — This had nothing do —

HOLLY. And does it mean you're rolling in the green and can quit that soul-mangling job of yours?

FRED. It doesn't pay *money.*

HOLLY. Don't do it.

FRED. No — it's — a very high-*toned* journal — this is how everybody started — Hemingway and Sherwood Anderson and Thornton Wilder — all of us. You *see?* Be happy for me.

HOLLY. ... I am, darling. You know what you ought to do? Throw the day away like so much trash. Just pick somebody up and get blotto and make a clamor in the streets and steal things!

FRED. Yes! I want to! *(Pause.)* What are you doing today?

HOLLY. Oh. *(Beat.)* Fred darling? I'm buying you lunch.

FRED. *(To us.)* What's more, it was October. If it were possible, I would go to live in one of those movies about prep school where it's October and October and October then she leaves him and for a few minutes it's November and then it goes back to being October. We hithered and yonned through the light, swift, amber, granular day. We ate. We drank. We stole. These: *(They take out cheap masks and put them on.)* I'm always meaning to make full restitution to Woolworth's now that I can *afford* the twenty-six cents.

## Scene 15

*Brooklyn Bridge. Light changes to early evening. They take off the masks.*

FRED. Then we found ourselves on the Brooklyn Bridge. Together in the slowing mellow evening, agog and quiet and city-struck. *(And this really must be gorgeous. Lovers both live and shadow, idling. The strung lights of the bridge.)* So lovely an hour that even Miss Holiday Golightly Traveling paused to wonder about things.

HOLLY. Talk to me about yourself.

FRED. About *me?*

HOLLY. Yes.

FRED. Why?

HOLLY. So as to make the quiet go away.

FRED. My Dickensian childhood, for example?

HOLLY. Start there why not.

FRED. I told her of my Dickensian childhood. Southern gothic they call it now, all oddness and rapture and neglect. Remember: I was a young, young, *young* man. I was wooing her with misery. Oh! I expected her cold gaze to melt and those defensive arms to be flung around my neck. For how could she resist the wounded and tender and deserving fellow I was showing myself to be?

HOLLY. Well, that certainly took the fizz out of the evening.

FRED. ... I ... didn't intend it to.

HOLLY. What *did* you intend?

FRED. I thought ... Some of that story might be familiar to you. I had this idea that you'd lived it yourself.

HOLLY. Nn-nn, sorry darling. I know your sweet cliché of a heart has me down as a waif but wasn't that way at all. My parents were nice and scatty. And there was plenty of food and twinkling lights and in winter the pond would freeze over and we'd skate on it and eat baked potatoes wrapped in foil —

FRED. — And you never went anywhere without your two best friends, Lady Diana Manners and Rebecca of Sunnybrook Farm.

HOLLY. Oh do you *know* Becky? Quel drip!

FRED. What about leaving home at fourteen?

HOLLY. All right. *That* part's true; the other wasn't — but my *God*, who could compete with that tale of woe you told in more time than it took to live it?

FRED. ... Huh. *(Then the bridge becomes curiously present. Two sets of lovers, one kissing, one just very close. And the light reaching its final intensity before yielding to the dark. Fred is as if stricken suddenly, complicated feelings play over his face. He pulls Holly to himself and kisses her.)*

HOLLY. People do such silly things in a mixed light.

FRED. Not so silly.

HOLLY. What is this, darling? Junior year a broad?

FRED. I don't know what you're —

HOLLY. *Those* gentlemen are in uniform, why aren't you?

FRED. ... Asthma runs in my family.

HOLLY. And it ran right past you, didn't it? Oh, darling Fred, lie to me if you have to but don't lie to yourself.

FRED. I'm not ... just one thing. *(Giddy-silly.)* I contain multitudes!

HOLLY. Well I *am* one thing and young men of limited means and unlimited confusion have no part in it.

FRED. Who does? Rusty Trawler?

HOLLY. What have you got against Rusty?

FRED. What do *you* love about him? His treasonous politics?

HOLLY. What *is* this about, really, Fred? It can't be simple distaste for poor dear Rusty.

FRED. Poor, dear Rusty is an amoral cretin with, no doubt, a predilection for violent amusements I don't even want to think about; doubtless, under your soignée ensembles, you're concealing scars from a raft of playful batterings.

HOLLY. I can assure you I'm not and stop acting some sort of angry disappointed suitor. Stop pretending you're something you're not. Stop pretending you ...

FRED. Oh, Holly Golightly, what a conventional woman you are! *(Beat.)*

HOLLY. What?

FRED. What a *phony*! What a pretender.

HOLLY. *Darling.*

FRED. Why did we come to this city if all our categories are intact?

HOLLY. I knew you had too much wine at lunch; I thought to stop you, but you were so charming.

FRED. Not too much.

HOLLY. Yes.

FRED. Not *enough*. Listen, listen … listen: My story is being published.

HOLLY. I know that.

FRED. And the night … is exquisite … and … something needs to be *done* about it!

HOLLY. Fred.

FRED. I don't want … jobs in cubbyholes and dry-cleaning and counting pennies and plans and definitions and saving up against whatever catastrophe's about to drop. I want … this moment, and this moment, and this moment. Look around *you* — how gorgeous it is — and you're *equal* to it and we've *found* each other so … why must things be brought to a halt? Because you "are" and I'm "not"! — It's — nonsense!

HOLLY. Darling —

FRED. It's —

HOLLY. Listen to me Fred. Listen *closely*.

FRED. But —

HOLLY. Listen: You're a neighbor that I'm fond of; that's as near to a friend as I can afford to have right now so don't go wrecking it with these *feelings* you're so intent on having. No good will come of them. Got that? I have plans and *you're* not *them*.

FRED. I — *(Realizes he has no thought to complete.)*

HOLLY. If you want to console yourself for the lost evening, you might try doing it with *that* — *(By which she means a sailor all by himself, staring fetchingly out at the water.)* No need to worry about abandoning me, either; I'm a girl who knows how to handle herself on a bridge.

FRED. *(Considers it.)* Let's just go home, all right?

HOLLY. All right. *(They walk. He puts the mask on again.)* Idiot.


# Scene 16


FRED. *(To us.)* November was not brief and did not yield to a second October. I don't remember December, except that it was listless and hopeless and I was largely drunk and Christmas came and of course Holly had a party. *(A party at Holly's.)*

HOLLY. Darling, you look like hell.

FRED. I aspire to hell.

HOLLY. I saw your story in that eso*te*ric magazine.

FRED. Oh, that was you?

HOLLY. I thought it looked very handsome, all printed up and real. Has it led to all sorts of things? *(He looks at her.)* I have something that might cheer you.

## Scene 17

*She takes him by the hand, the party flares, and they are in her bedroom. She presents him with the birdcage.*

HOLLY. For you, *mon ange.*

FRED. Holly! This is dreadful!

HOLLY. I quite agree. But you were lusting after it so.

FRED. No — it's magnificent, but the *cost* —

HOLLY. Oh — a few extra trips to the loo. Just promise me you'll never put a living thing in it. Swear.

FRED. I swear. All I got you is this: *(He presents her with a St. Christopher medallion.)* It's St. Christopher — Patron saint of travelers.

HOLLY. Oh, Fred, I'll treasure it always.

FRED. You'll have lost it by Saturday.

HOLLY. But *till* then.

FRED. It's from Tiffany's.

HOLLY. Bless you, darling. *(She hugs him. Jose enters.)*

JOSE. Holly, I — *(Sees the two of them.)* Oh! I am so sorry. I came because ... I was looking for ...

HOLLY. Oh — yes! ... It isn't here.

JOSE. Well then ... I ... *(Mag enters.)*

MAG. Sugar, where are you hidin'? Why aren't you at the party? *(Sees the group: Jose and Holly looking vaguely caught; Fred vaguely enjoying it.)* My! It certainly is crowded here. *(Baleful.)* Whatch'all doin'? *(Fred exits with birdcage.)*

# Scene 18

*Fred returns to his room. He hangs the birdcage from some sort of ceiling hook, fan blade, or light fixture or whatever. He falls onto his bed, staring at the ceiling. He stares up at the birdcage, which gives off an intensely golden glow.*

*Hold like that. Then: Holly's back in her apartment, in a bathing suit, under a sun lamp. Fred joins her.*

FRED. Two weeks passed when Holly was nowhere to be found. Then as mysteriously as she disappeared, she returned. *(To Holly.)* Have you been hibernating?

HOLLY. Oh God, I've had to make myself scarce — it's been a hellish time Chez Golightly.

FRED. Tell.

HOLLY. *Some*how Mag has got it into that rump brain of hers that Jose and I are sleeping together!

FRED. No! How did she conceive such a far-fetched notion?

HOLLY. Haven't a clue but it was pretty touch-and-go until I finally sat her down for a real heart-to-heart.

FRED. And you convinced her?

HOLLY. God, *yes.*

FRED. How?

HOLLY. I told her I was a lesbian.

FRED. She didn't believe that — she couldn't.

HOLLY. She's sleeping on a cot now.

FRED. You're stupendous.

HOLLY. *(Yes, but bored by it.)* I suppose. Be a darling, darling, rub some oil on my back. *(He does.)* O.J.'s in town.

FRED. … Oh?

HOLLY. I gave him your story in the magazine.

FRED. Uh-huh.

HOLLY. He was quite impressed.

FRED. Was he?

HOLLY. He thinks maybe you're worth helping.

FRED. Oh my — like the poor.

HOLLY. But he says you're on the wrong track. Negroes and children: Who cares?

FRED. Not Mr. Berman I take it.

HOLLY. Well, I agree with him. I read that story twice. Trembling leaves. *Description.* It doesn't mean anything. *(He lifts his flattened oiling hand as if to hit her, then comes down oiling. Pause.)*

FRED. Give me an example of something that *means* something. In your opinion.

HOLLY. *Wuthering Heights.*

FRED. *Wuthering Heights*! But that's pure unexampled genius! You can't expect me to —

HOLLY. It was, wasn't it? "My wild, sweet Cathy." I cried buckets. I saw it ten times.

FRED. Oh ... oh. *(With a scornful laugh.)* The movie.

HOLLY. *(Rigid.)* Everybody has to feel superior to somebody. But it's customary to present a little proof before you take the privilege.

FRED. I don't compare myself to you. Or Berman. Therefore I can't feel superior. We want different things.

HOLLY. Don't you want to make money?

FRED. I haven't planned that far.

HOLLY. That's how your stories sound. As though you'd written them without knowing the end. Well I'll tell you: You'd better make money. You have an expensive imagination. Not many people are going to buy you bird cages. *(Beat.)*

FRED. Oh. *(Beat.)* How funny! I'd not realized that the birdcage ... was made of money. Or that ... I was somehow ... its equivalent in dollars, but one time only or ... something ... I'd thought somehow that it was an expression of some kind of ... *So* sorry.

HOLLY. You *will* be if you hit me.

FRED. *Hit* you?

HOLLY. You wanted to a minute ago. I could feel it in your hand.

FRED. ... Ah.

HOLLY. And you want to now. I shouldn't give in. You'll regret it if you do.

FRED. *(Entire body straining to lash out at her.)* Oh no, I wouldn't regret that. I'm only sorry you wasted your money on me: Rusty Trawler is too hard a way of earning it.

HOLLY. *(Quiet seething.)* People who live in glass whorehouses, darling —

FRED. I have *never* done what — I have never *sunk* to the level of — *(He stops himself, horrified.)*

HOLLY. *(Sits up.)* It should take you about four seconds to walk from here to the door. I'll give you two.

## Scene 19

*He leaves. He storms into his room, takes down the birdcage. He plops it down defiantly in front of Holly's apartment, returns to his room. He sits in his chair.*

*Time passes.*

*He returns to the hall outside Holly's apartment, retrieves the birdcage, hangs it up again.*

*Holly's apartment. A party. Loud, exorbitant, crowded, bereft of Fred. He sits staring out, lonely.*

*Madame Spanella appears.*

MADAME SPANELLA. *(Straight out, but for Fred.)* Look at you: *sola, perduta, abbandonata.* Now perhaps you will sign my petition. I have drafted it in the cause of evicting the whore Holly Golightly. These are the grounds: Moral Iniquity. Behavior Inappropriate to a Building Over Fifty Years of Age. Inhuman and Detestable Noise. The Harboring of Vagrants and General Destruction of Peace of Mind. Perhaps you have charges of your *own* you'd like to add. There's room.

FRED. No, those are ample.

MADAME SPANELLA. *(Proffers pen.)* Then you will sign?

FRED. ... No.

MADAME SPANELLA. *Bambini, bambini, bambini. (The party grows louder and brighter. The cacophony propels him into the street. An image that conveys a mood of exquisite romantic loneliness: The Sinatra album covers from ten years later.)*

FRED. *(To us.)* My happy New Year inventory: Unfriended, with a job that smothered me, a writing life too stagnant to be called a career, and as if all this wasn't enough, I was being pursued. *(A long, lean, old country fellow appears, eyes on Fred.)* It was gradual, like becoming aware that you had a mouse. First a nameless disquiet. Then sounds. Then the creature itself hove into view. I thought: *This* man wants me? Do I look *that* bad?

## Scene 20

*Hamburg Heaven comes into view: a sign and a counter. Fred seats himself at a stool, is served a burger. The man enters, sits on the stool next to his.*

FRED. *(To us.)* Youth is often mistaken for a panoply of other qualities — beauty, hunger, availability. But the mingled aromas of sweat and tobacco and decrepitude have never been my call to venereal action and as this man and I stared at each other in the mirror that ran the length of the counter, I ... finally: *(To man.)* Excuse me — but what do you want?

MAN. Son, I need a friend.

FRED. I thought as much. Well, sorry, I am not going to *be* that — *(The man has removed snapshot from wallet.)*

MAN. Take a look. *(Fred looks. Image: seven, frankly, hillbillies. Frayed, faded Walker Evans.)* That's me. That's Lulamae. That's her brother Fred.

FRED. My God — you're Holly's father.

MAN. No, son, I'm not her father.

FRED. Then —

MAN. I'm her husband. *(Extends hand.)* Doc Golightly. Pleased to make your acquaintance.

## End of Act One

# ACT TWO

## Scene 1

*Hamburg Heaven. Fred is with Doc.*

DOC. Her name's not Holly. She was a Lulamae Barnes. Was till she married me. I'm a horse doctor, animal man. Do some farmin' too. Near Tulip, Texas. Son, why are you laughin'?

FRED. I'm ... not. Actually.

DOC. This here's no humorous matter, son. I'm a tired man. I've been five years lookin' for my woman. Soon as I got that letter from Fred sayin' where she was, I bought myself a ticket on the Greyhound. Lulamae belongs home with her husband and her churren.

FRED. Children?

DOC. *(Re: the photo.)* Them's her churren.

FRED. You're deranged. Holly can't be the mother of those children; they're older than she is — they're *bigger* than —

DOC. Now son, I didn't claim they were her natural-born churren. Their own precious mother, precious woman, Jesus rest her soul, she passed away July 4th, Independence Day, the year of the drought. When I married Lulamae she promised to be my wife and the mother of my churren. Now son, do you doubt me? Do you believe what I'm saying is so?

FRED. I ... *(Surprised.)* do...

DOC. Plain broke our hearts when she ran off like she done. She had no cause. All the housework was done by her daughters. Lulamae could just take it easy: fuss in front of mirrors and wash her hair. Our own cows, our own garden, chickens, pigs: Son, that woman got positively fat. While her brother growed into a giant. Which is a sight different from how they come to us.

FRED. Please tell me: How *did* they come to you?

DOC. 'Twas Nellie, my oldest girl, 'twas Nellie brought them into the house. She come to me one morning and said: "Papa, I got two wild young-uns locked in the kitchen. I caught 'em outside stealing milk and turkey eggs." That was Lulamae and Fred. Well, you never saw a more pitiful something. Ribs sticking out everywhere, legs so puny they can't hardly stand, teeth wobbling so badly they can't chew mush. Story was: Their mother died of the TB, and their papa done the same — and all the churren, a whole raft of 'em, they been sent off to live with different mean people. Now Lulamae and her brother, them two been living with some mean, no-count people a hundred miles east of Tulip. She had good cause to run off from that house. She didn't have none to leave mine. 'Twas her home. She plumped out to be a real pretty woman. Lively, too. Talky as a jaybird. With something smart to say on every subject: better than the radio. First thing you know, I'm out picking flowers. I tamed her a crow and taught it to say her name. I showed her how to play the guitar. Just to look at her made the tears spring to my eyes. The night I proposed, I cried like a baby. She said: "What you want to cry for, Doc? 'Course we'll be married. I've never been married before." Well, I had to laugh: *never been married before*! Don't tell me that woman wasn't happy! We all doted on her. She didn't have to lift a finger 'cept to eat a piece of pie. 'Cept to comb her hair and send away for all the magazines. We must've had a hunnerd dollars worth of magazine come into that house. Ask me, that's what done it. Looking at show-off pictures. Reading dreams. That's what started her walking down the road. Every day she'd walk a little further: a mile, and come home. Two miles, and come home. One day she just kept on. The crow I give her went wild and flew away. All summer you could hear him. In the yard. In the garden. In the woods. All summer that damned bird was calling: Lulamae, Lulamae … I know she's sorry for what she done. I know she wants to go home.

FRED.  I think you'll find Holly — Lulamae, rather — somewhat changed.

DOC.  Listen son, I advised you I need a friend. Because I don't want to surprise her. Scare her none. That's why I've held off. Be my friend: Let her know I'm here. (*Fred considers this possibility. It tempts him for unkind reasons. He yields.*)

FRED.  Certainly, *cer*tainly I'll be your friend, Mr. —

DOC.  Doc.

FRED.  Doc. (*Doc straightens his tie, brushes his sleeves.*)

DOC.  Do I look nice?

FRED.  Nicer than anyone Lulamae's seen in years.

## Scene 2

*Fred climbs to Holly's door. Holly answers in full party regalia.*

HOLLY. Well, idiot. I'm in too much of a hurry to make up now. We'll smoke the pipe tomorrow, okay?

FRED. Sure, Lulamae. If you're still around tomorrow. *(Beat.)*

HOLLY. *He* told you that! Oh please. *Where* is he? Fred! Fred! Where are you darling. *(She rushes down and out. Doc appears. She recoils in disappointment.)*

DOC. Gosh Lulamae. Gee honey, don't they feed you up here? You're so skinny. Like when I first saw you. All wild around the eye.

HOLLY. Hello, Doc. *(She touches his chin, almost to feel that he's real.)* Hello, Doc. *(She kisses him on the cheek. Doc lifts her off the ground and she laughs.)*

DOC. Gosh, Lulamae. Kingdom come. *(Madame Spanella appears.)*

MADAME SPANELLA. *This* man! She must be charging half-price. *(Fred watches, astounded and bereaved, as Doc carries Holly into her apartment. He walks, dejected, to:)*

## Scene 3

*Joe's bar. Fred and Yunioshi seated, drinking and glum, Joe serving them.*

JOE. How is it you never come in here with the other writers?

FRED. I'm not so keen on writers, as a class.

JOE. No?

FRED. No. Don't like 'em.

JOE. Let me tell you somethin', buddy boy. I've been havin' writers in this place goin' on twenty years — and none of 'em has ever liked any of 'em. Ya know what they do instead?

FRED. Tell me.

JOE. Befriend 'em.

FRED. Ah! *(Yunioshi makes a noise.)*

JOE. What's your beef, Yunioshi?

YUNIOSHI. I am disgusted with myself.

JOE. That's new.

YUNIOSHI. Yesterday, I shot a cover for *Vogue* magazine. The image was in the highest style: A starving woman dressed as a dead bird. It will cause enormous amounts of money to be spent. I am a pimp for the American economy while in California my cousins mill about in pens, like pigs. That is why I am disgusted with myself.

FRED. This war, this *damn*able war. *(Beat.)* Also, it can be very hard to get a cab. *(Yunioshi looks at him, livid — Bolts his drink, drops change on counter, exits.)* Do you think, Joe, that I am insufficiently cognizant of the nuances of the political situation? Because I sometimes think that I am insufficiently cog —

JOE. I think you're a young guy who hasn't gotten a hold of what he wants yet. Not enough of it anyway, and not fast enough, where's other young guys have. And it makes you want to be mean to people sometimes.

FRED. You are a very sagacious fellow, Joseph Bell. But do you know, Joe, do you know what is worse than not wanting other people to have what you want?

JOE. What?

FRED. Not wanting other people to have ... what you *don't* want.

JOE. ... I'll take your word for it. *(Holly enters.)*

FRED. Enter Miss Lulamae Barnes. Fresh as a daisy, or should that be "Tulip"?

HOLLY. Don't be a beast. Set me up, would you, Joe? The girl's in a state.

FRED. *(To us.)* Two drinks later:

HOLLY. *Divorce* him? Of course I never divorced him. I was only a child, for God's sake. It couldn't have been *legal. (Tapping martini glass.)* Two more, my darling Mr. Bell.

JOE. You're rockin' the boat kinda early.

HOLLY. But it's Sunday, Mr. Bell. Clocks are slow on Sunday. Besides, I haven't been to bed yet. *(Whispers to Fred.)* Not to sleep.

FRED. You are ... limitless, aren't —

HOLLY. Well, I had to. Doc really loves me, you know. And I love him. He may have looked old and tacky to *you*. But you don't know the sweetness of him, the confidence he can give to birds and brats and fragile things like that. Anyone who ever gave you confidence, you owe them a lot. Oh! I must look fierce. But who wouldn't? We spent the rest of the night roaming around in a bus station. Right up till the last minute Doc thought I was going to go with him. *(Doc appears.)*

DOC. We'll fatten you up Lulamae; it'll be just like the old days.

HOLLY. But, Doc, these aren't the old days and I'm not Lulamae any more.

DOC. To me you are.

HOLLY. And the terrible part is, I am. I realized it standing there. I'm still stealing turkey eggs and running through a briar patch. Only now I call it having the mean reds.

JOE. Your third round. And on the record: I'm against it.

DOC. The bus is here, Lulamae. Time to climb aboard.

HOLLY. Doc, I'm not going with you!

DOC. 'Course you are. This bus is headed for where we live. It's headed for home. *(Beat.)*

HOLLY. You're always taking in wild things, Doc. A hawk with a hurt wing. That full-grown bobcat with a broken leg. But you can't give your heart to a wild thing; the more you do, the stronger they get. Until they're strong enough to run into the woods. Or fly into a tree. Then a taller tree. Then the sky.

DOC. The churren, they —

HOLLY. *(Holds her hand to him.)* Thank you, Doc. For everything you've given me. Thank you sincerely. *(After a moment, he takes it. They embrace.)*

DOC. Good luck, Lulamae.

HOLLY. Goodbye, Doc. *(She watches him go.)* Never love a wild thing, Mr. Bell. You'll end up looking at the sky.

JOE. She's drunk.

FRED. Indeed.

HOLLY. *(Lifts her glass.)* Let's wish Doc luck, too. *(Clinks with Fred.)* Good luck, dearest Doc. And believe me — it's better to look at the sky than to live there. Such an empty place; so vague. Just a country where the thunder goes and things disappear. *(She drinks. She gazes out. Light shift.)*

FRED. *(To us.)* And soon the mean reds would be general all over New York.

## Scene 4

*Image: Eustace Tilley. Stern Lady Boss sits in her office. Fred enters.*

FRED. I was told you want to see me. *(SLB is writing something, doesn't respond.)* ... I got — re*ceiv*ed a message that you ... want —

SLB. Ah. Yes. Sit.

FRED. *(Sits.)* I haven't done anything wrong, I hope ... *(SLB continues writing.)* I haven't done anything wrong, have I? Disappointed in some way? Because —

SLB. *(Abrupt.)* Why are you hostile to the semi-colon?

FRED. ... Pardon?

SLB. The semi-colon. Why do you disdain it so?

FRED. ... I am not aware of any par*tic*ular —

SLB. Then why do you persist in your failure to master its usage?

FRED. I'll have to discuss that with my shrink, I guess; ha-ha.

SLB. If I thought it was stupidity —

FRED. I certainly will *try* —

SLB. And perhaps it *is* —

FRED. I don't *think* —

SLB. In any event, this is not school, I am not your headmaster; your tutelage is not my business, nor is your ultimate success in life my responsibility. You are not a statistic that will reflect on this magazine one way or the other. It is my sad duty to inform you that you are no longer in our employ.

FRED. I will apply myself to an in*ten*sive study of the semi —

SLB. There are other reasons.

FRED. *What* other?

SLB. We shall not speak of them.

FRED. May I ask why?

SLB. It involves the supply room — the proper usage of which you seem to understand as little as you do that of the semi-colon. *(Fred stops, realizes. Blushes. SLB, dryly:)* Yes.

FRED. Listen, um. It's rather difficult these days to find the sort of job exactly suited to my abilities and my exchequer is a tad bereft of —

SLB. You should have thought of that before you ...

45

FRED. So while I realize that in cases such as this, dismissal is routine, I was wondering if I could beseech you to make an exception just this one time.

SLB. Exceptions are for the exceptional. *(He stops talking.)* Good luck to you. *(He goes out, is lost. Lights dim on him. Perhaps he makes a call at a pay phone.)*

## Scene 5

*Meanwhile at Holly's — Morning. Holly and Jose enter in evening clothes.*

JOSE. Did you know? Rusty has explained it to me once.

HOLLY. Explained it?

JOSE. That you are his one great love.

HOLLY. *(Gravely.)* He *told* you that? I see.

JOSE. And that he is yours. In such a way that no one could ever come between you.

HOLLY. So. The truth is out. Oh darling, I'm perfectly *raddled* with shame. *Can* you forgive me?

JOSE. It came as a great shock.

HOLLY. Yes?

JOSE. *(Shrugs.)* But whatever must be must be. Meantime, I am a man of the world.

HOLLY. Bless you, darling. And, of course, the *world. (They laugh, are at each other. They sink onto the bed. Lights dim on them.)*

# Scene 6

*Fred and Editor in an alley. Editor has a tabloid folded under his arm.*

FRED. I'm very grateful that you —
EDITOR. No — no — no need to be *gra*teful. Still think you're a most interesting young writer —
FRED. I'm glad —
EDITOR. Liked the story in uh in uh —
FRED. Thank you; I *hop*ed you would. Well, as I said, I'm without a means of support for the moment and I — By the way, do you *always* conduct your business meetings in darkened alleyways and before proper business hours?
EDITOR. I uh — this is uh — spot of air.
FRED. If that much. Well ... *(Moves a little closer.)* I thought ... we got on pretty well ... and I'm willing to do any kind of labor that pays a scant wage — a *dec*ent wage.
EDITOR. I see, I see. The thing is ... while I *like* your work and would *like* to support your promise, word got round about that ... episode.
FRED. I was let go because of my neglect of the semi-colon, a grammatical oversight I've since remedied.
EDITOR. As I understand it, the semi-colon wasn't the problem. *(Beat. Fred sighs.)*
FRED. Listen. Look. Listen ... I haven't been having much luck finding something in my line. So, *if* ... you ...
EDITOR. In a few months, when it's all been forgotten ... perhaps then? We're a family house, you know, essentially wholesome. Despite the occasional Euro*pe*an novel. *(He places a hand apologetically on Fred's cheek, withdraws it quickly.)* Well ... Goodbye to you. *(Waves a crisp farewell with newspaper.)*
FRED. *(Seeing headline.)* Wait! Give me your paper!
EDITOR. But —
FRED. *Give me your paper! (Editor hands it over, exits quickly. Reads headline.)* No! *(Image: Tabloid cover — "Rusty Trawler weds.")*

## Scene 7

*Holly's: Holly is finishing dressing, calls to Jose offstage.*

HOLLY. Darling, make some coffee, would you? That lovely Brazilian sludge of yours if we've got the beans. *(Jose enters.)*
JOSE. There's been a telegram. *(Holly looks at him, curious. Takes it.)*
FRED. *(Reads the tabloid.)* "Continued on Page 6." *(He gets to the page. Image: "Trawler marries Wildwood." A stunned moment. Then he laughs. Then, tumultuously, lights down on him. Holly's: She opens the telegram. She reads it, Jose looking on. For a moment she's terrifyingly still. Then she starts to tremble. Then lets out a sound, almost inhuman. She lunges blindly at what? Jose grabs her.)*
JOSE. Holly!

## Scene 8

*The scene changes physically. Hallway. Madame Spanella and Yunioshi converge. Holly screaming off.*

YUNIOSHI. Miss Golightly — please — may we help you —
MADAME SPANELLA. Whoring! Murder! Violence — I kn*ew* it would come to this —
YUNIOSHI. Please — may we get some help — *(Fred enters.)*
FRED. What's happening?
YUNIOSHI. She won't let us in —
MADAME SPANELLA. She is murdering someone; someone is murdering her!
YUNIOSHI. I think she's alone; this started some time ago, I don't know what has —
MADAME SPANELLA. Call the police! Murder! *Mur*der! *(Fred elbows past them to outside Holly's apartment.)*

48

FRED. Holly! Holly, it's me! Let me in. Let me in please!

MADAME SPANELLA. Death! *Vi*olence!

FRED. *Shut up!* Holly! *(He tries to ram his way in, is only wounded.)*

YUNIOSHI. Shall I call someone? Do you know? Is there anyone to call? *(Jose enters, accompanied by a man: Dr. Goldman.)*

JOSE. *(Stern and nervous.)* Out of my way, please. *(He uses his key to open the door.)*

MADAME SPANELLA. Has she gone mad?

JOSE. Go away. In here, Dr. Goldman.

MADAME SPANELLA. I *said* we should evict her! I *said* so!

JOSE. Away!

YUNIOSHI. *(Gesturing her to leave with him.)* Please. Be decent.


# Scene 9


*Mr. Yunioshi leaves. Madame Spanella retreats but only a little. Jose and the doctor enter the apartment. It is trashed. Fred enters too, but stays at a distance. Holly is moaning, low and steady. The doctor approaches.*


DR. GOLDMAN. Miss Golightly? I'm Dr. Goldman. *(She neither acknowledges him nor resists. He sits beside her. Takes her pulse.)* You're a tired young lady. Very tired. You want to go to sleep, don't you? Sleep.

HOLLY. Sleep. He's the only one would ever let me. Let me hug him on cold nights. I saw a place in Mexico. With horses by the sea.

DR. GOLDMAN. *(Lullabying while inserting hypodermic.)* With horses by the sea.

JOSE. *(Averting face, queasy.)* Her sickness is only grief. She is grieving, only?

DR. GOLDMAN. *(Cotton swab.)* Didn't hurt a bit now, did it?

HOLLY. *Everything* hurts. Where are my glasses? *(She's drifting off.)*

JOSE. She is only grieving?

DR. GOLDMAN. Please, sir. If you will leave me alone with the patient. *(Jose and Fred move into front room. Madame Spanella snoops there.)*

49

JOSE. What are you doing? What are you doing, woman? *(He unleashes a cavalcade of Spanish oaths.)*

MADAME SPANELLA. Don't touch me! I'll call the police! *(She backs out.)*

JOSE. A drink, perhaps?

FRED. Yes ... yes.

JOSE. ... All the bottles ... appear to be broken.

FRED. We don't need to drink. *(Jose smiles slightly, obscurely grateful.)*

JOSE. I have a worry that this should cause scandal. Her crashing everything. Conducting herself like a crazy woman. I must have no public scandal. It is too delicate: my name, my work.

FRED. Demolishing one's own possessions seems a private affair; I can't imagine a scandal coming of it.

JOSE. It is only a question of grieving. When the sadness came, first she throws the drink she is drinking. The bottles. A lamp. Then I am scared. I hurry to bring a doctor.

FRED. But why? Why should she have a fit over Rusty? If I were her, I'd celebrate.

JOSE. Rusty? Oh, that! They do us a grand favor, Rusty and Mag. We laugh over it: How they think they break our hearts when all the time we *want* them to run away. I assure you, we were laughing when the sadness came. This. *(He hands Fred a telegram.)*

FRED. *(Reads.)* "Received notice young Fred killed in action overseas stop your family joins in the sorrow of our mutual loss stop letter follows love Doc." *(Fred goes to Holly, sits beside her. She reaches for him. He holds her.)*

HOLLY. *(Murmurs.)* Fred ... *(Jose looks on. Fred detaches.)*

## Scene 10

*Image: a page from Fred's diary.*

FRED. *(To us.)* These last weeks: torment and paralysis and tragedy and humiliation ... and something else. Holly has been extraordinary. *(Holly rises from the bed, transforms. Pins back her hair, wipes off her makeup. Puts on, maybe, a sweatshirt, becomes simple and calm.)* Grief hasn't changed so much as simplified her. She no longer calls me

Fred. She says:

HOLLY. *(Offstage.)* We need to find you a *new* name, darling.

FRED. "What about my real one?" I ask her.

HOLLY. *(Offstage.)* Haven't decided what that is yet.

FRED. Mostly, she calls me "darling." *(Holly, meanwhile, has set up house. She's cooking. A Portuguese instruction record plays. Fred joins her.)*

HOLLY. *Tenho muito prazer em conhecê-lo. ("I'm very glad to meet you.")* Who ever dreamed I would be such a marvelous cook? It seems I have a natural talent. And just think, a few months ago, I couldn't even scramble eggs.

FRED. *(Pouring himself a drink.)* You still can't.

HOLLY. *Dar*ling.

FRED. Or broil a steak or make a proper salad. Simplicity eludes you.

HOLLY. Nonsense.

FRED. What's for dinner tonight?

HOLLY. A perfectly mundane roast pheasant with pomegranate and persimmon sauce.

FRED. Again?

HOLLY. Well, I'm sure it's mundane in Portugal. Among the Gran*dees* or whatever they call themselves.

FRED. Is Jose in Washington?

HOLLY. Just the two of us tonight.

FRED. Good.

HOLLY. *(Sitting opposite him.)* The pheasant's cooking on its own; we can tuck in and have a nice chat. *(She's knitting.)*

FRED. My God, who *is* this woman?

HOLLY. Little Holly: happy at last.

FRED. "At last." Hm.

HOLLY. But how are you?

FRED. Oh — How should a male librarian be in high summer.

HOLLY. You're not a librarian forever — or at *all*, really, just a temporary clerk.

FRED. *(To us.)* This was the job I had landed after — oh forget it. *(To her.)* Yes: temporary.

HOLLY. You have only yourself to thank for losing the last situation. You did it on purpose, you know; any halfway decent Freudian could tell you that; it was a plea to be fired, a cri de cœur, that travesty.

FRED. I shouldn't have told you. Remind me never again to drink in your vicinity. *(He takes a swig.)*

HOLLY. And in the supply room!

FRED. I had a need; he supplied it.

HOLLY. I never tire of that joke, darling. *(He smiles abashedly.)* Did you love him?

FRED. Oh please.

HOLLY. That's not an answer.

FRED. He made no secret of his opinion that *he* was destined for glory, whereas I, if I were lucky, would one day be promoted to chief assistant copy editor. Yes, subconsciously, it *was* all about getting fired — getting *him* fired. I *loathed* him.

HOLLY. Do you miss him?

FRED. *(Sheepish.)* Only a little ... It's nice this. The two of us. Pleasant to have Jose gone, isn't it?

HOLLY. Yes. And it's pleasant to have him here.

FRED. But less so.

HOLLY. For *you.*

FRED. Do *you* love *him*?

HOLLY. Of course I do. Please don't laugh at me — but I wish I'd been a virgin for him. *(Fred laughs.)* It's not *that* hilarious. It's not as if I've warmed the multitudes the way some claim I have. I toted it up the other night, and I've only had eleven lovers — not counting anything that happened before I was thirteen because, well, that just doesn't count. Eleven — does that make me a whore? Look at Mag. Or Honey Tucker. They've had the ol' clap-yo-hand so many times it amounts to applause. Oh, I do loves Jose. He's ... *friendly.* He can laugh me out of the mean reds, only I don't have them much anymore, except sometimes. And even then they're not so hideola that I gulp Seconal and have to haul myself to Tiffany's. I take his suit to the cleaner's or stuff some mushrooms and I feel just great.

FRED. *(Stiffly.)* I'm glad.

HOLLY. I'll miss it all of course. Somewhat. I was on the Brooklyn Bridge the other day watching the ships and I imagined that they were bringing me back here. Isn't that funny? That's how on to the next thing I am. I saw the picture clear as clear — me and my nine Brazilian brats gazing at the tall lady's armpit. Because, *yes,* they *must* see this city — the lights, the river —

FRED. But this is all a pipe dream. *(Beat. But Holly is strangely calm, unoffended.)*

HOLLY. It isn't, though, darling. Jose is terribly real. Hell, I've even taught myself to cook for the man.

FRED. That has its costs; you've put on weight.

HOLLY. I'm going to be putting on a great deal more weight in very short order. I'm preggers. *(Pause. They look at each other. Silence. He stands there.)*

FRED. Do you mind if I turn this damned record off? It's making me about insane. *(He goes to it. Makes a gesture to take it off, we hear the scratch of the needle. He stands there.)*

HOLLY. I'll think of you, darling, from time to time, when I'm in Rio or wherever, all plump and happy and swaddled in young-uns.

FRED. Really — don't.

HOLLY. No way around it. You've left your mark on me *that* much. *(Racketing noise.)*

## Scene 11

FRED. This part begins ... Oh God, how *does* it begin? *(Takes a breath, narrates.)* It begins with a day unlike any I'd ever known.

HOLLY. Darling, come with me. I need to see a horse about a man.

FRED. Pardon?

HOLLY. Because of a man at any rate. Mabel Minerva. I can't go without saying goodbye to my darling Mabel Minerva.

FRED. "Goodbye"? What means "goodbye"?

HOLLY. Jose bought the tickets. I leave a week from Saturday.

FRED. *(As if the words aren't words.)* ... A week ... from Saturday?

HOLLY. Yes.

FRED. But a week from Saturday ... *exists*. I mean, it's a real calendar *day*.

HOLLY. I know that darling. Isn't it marvelous?

FRED. How long will you be gone?

HOLLY. Eternally.

FRED. That's not possible —

HOLLY. But it is

FRED. Look, you can't just ... upsticks and leave. Think of all the people who'll miss you.

HOLLY. Nobody will miss me.

FRED. Your *friends*!

HOLLY. *(Simply.)* I don't have any friends. *(Fred takes the blow. Almost reels from it, but won't give in.)*

53

FRED. Joe Bell! Sally Tomato — you have the weather report to give.
HOLLY. Haven't done that in weeks, there's some need to lay low. He had Mr. O'Shaughnessy present me with a five-hundred-dollar wedding gift in fact.
FRED. Has Jose actually proposed to you?
HOLLY. He's going to in Rio; don't worry your head about that.
FRED. Does he know your first marriage was never annulled?
HOLLY. Mention that to a living soul, darling, I'll hang you by your toes and dress you for a hog. Now. Are we riding or are you dead to me?
FRED. *(To us.)* The stables — I believe they've been replaced by television studios — were on West Sixty-seventh street. Holly selected for me an old sway-back mare.
HOLLY. Don't worry, she's safer than a cradle.


# Scene 12


*And I believe all this is accomplished through the simplest, prop-less mime. While the ride itself is a matter of projections.*


FRED. She'd *have* to be for me. *(They mount. Then ride, then the images tell us they start to take up a little speed and pass places at a gently accelerating pace.)*
HOLLY. See? It's great! *(Sound and projections: The day — crisp and beautiful and calm.)*
FRED. And suddenly it was. Suddenly, watching Holly's face in the red-yellow leaf light, I loved her enough to forget myself, my self-pitying despairs, and be content that something she thought happy was going to happen. Very gently the horses began to trot, waves of wind splashed us, spanked our faces, we plunged in and out of sun and shadow pools, and joy, a glad-to-be-alive exhilaration jolted through me like a jigger of nitrogen. That was one minute. And then: *(Several images: City urchins sporting sticks and rocks. Sounds of taunting, in English and Spanish. Fred begins to have trouble handling the horse.)* Stop that! Leave her alone! Stop. *(Images: Urchins switching and flicking at the horse. Horse starts bucking, Fred's balance starts to*

*go, he weaves.)* Holly, they're —

HOLLY. Yes, darling, I see. Stop that, you little brutes. Leave that sweet horse alone. *(They don't. A flip-book sequence of images of the urchins taunting and hitting. Fred totally loses control.)*

FRED. Oh! God!

HOLLY. Darling! *(Stage as you will but suddenly Fred is far downstage and Holly is far upstage and Fred is hanging on for dear life. Images: Horrified onlookers, nursemaids clutching their charges, bums cheering.)*

FRED. H-E-E-E-ELP!!!!

HOLLY. Hold on, darling! You've got her! You're in *charge,* darling!

FRED. *Charge!* Onto Fifth Avenue — *(Images: Traffic, taxis, buses swerving.)* Past the Duke Mansion, the Frick Museum, past the Pierre and the Plaza. *(Accelerated images.)* And finally: *(Fred veers, upheaves, falls to the ground. Holly rides up beside him, kneels.)*

HOLLY. Darling, how do you feel? *(Pause.)*

FRED. *(Disembodied voice.)* Fine.

HOLLY. *(Takes his wrist.)* But you haven't *any* pulse. *(Beat.)*

FRED. Then I must be dead.

HOLLY. Idiot. *(Carefully, she helps him up.)*

## Scene 13

*She walks him into his apartment, undresses him and herself, and helps him into the bathtub. Then joins him there. SFX: A siren. During this, typing sound and:*

REPORTER. Members of café society were stunned today by the arrest of gorgeous Holly Golightly, Hollywood starlet and highly-publicized girl-about-New York. At the same time, 2 P.M., police nabbed Oliver O'Shaughnessy, 52, of the Hotel Seabord, West Forty-ninth Street, as he exited from a Hamburg Heaven on Madison Avenue.

FRED. *(To us.)* Somehow, she got me home. And naked. And nursed me. It was perfect. Well I *thought* it was perfect.

REPORTER. Both are alleged by District Attorney Frank L. Donovan to be important figures in an international drug ring dominated by the notorious Mafia-führer Salvatore "Sally" Tomato, currently in Sing Sing serving a five-year rap for political bribery. *(Reporter continues typing.)*

HOLLY. How do you feel darling?

FRED. *(Loopy.)* I see two of you.

HOLLY. You're improving — in the cab you saw four.

FRED. What's that?

HOLLY. Liniment.

FRED. Nice.

REPORTER. Although the D.A.'s office has issued no formal statement, responsible sources insist the beautiful actress, not long ago the constant companion of multimillionaire Rutherfurd Trawler, has been acting as "liaison" between the imprisoned Tomato and his chief-lieutenant O'Shaughnessy.

HOLLY. We'll get all your kinks unkinked then into bed you go to sleep.

FRED. No — no bed — only this.

HOLLY. I can't keep doing this forever.

FRED. Just till we die.

REPORTER. Miss Golightly, who has no previous criminal record, was arrested in her luxurious apartment at a swank East Side address. *(Suddenly, Madame Spanella enters, followed by a bashful-looking male cop and a vaguely sadistic female one.)*

MADAME SPANELLA. *(Pointing.)* Here she is: the Wanted Woman!

HOLLY. What the *fuck*!

FRED. *(Simul.)* Is something happening?

MADAME SPANELLA. *(Enjoying the culpable nudity.)* Look. What a whore she is.

FEMALE COP. *(Manhandling her.)* Come along, sister, you're going places.

FRED. Jesus!

HOLLY. Get them cotton-pickin' hands off of me, you dreary, driveling old bull-dyke. *(Female cop slaps her. So hard that the liniment goes flying.)*

FRED. Hey! *(He scampers out of the tub, pratfalls on liniment spill. Cries out.)*

HOLLY. *(As they take her away.)* Darling — don't forget — please feed the cat! *(Fred dresses himself shakily as:)*

REPORTER. Talking to reporters outside the East Sixty-seventh Street Precinct Station, Miss Golightly, a fragile eyeful, appeared relatively unconcerned.

## Scene 14

*Holly appears, coat wrapped around her, outside precinct.*

HOLLY. Don't ask me what the hell this is about.
REPORTER. She told reporters.
HOLLY. *Parce que je ne sais pas, mes chers.*
REPORTER. "Because I do not know, my dears."
HOLLY. Yes — I have visited Sally Tomato. I used to go to see him every week. What's wrong with that? He believes in God and so do I. *(Subheading: Admits own drug addiction.)*
REPORTER. Miss Golightly, are you yourself a narcotics user?
HOLLY. I've had a little go at marijuana. It's not half so destructive as brandy. Cheaper, too. Unfortunately, I prefer brandy. No, Mr. Tomato never mentioned drugs to me. It makes me furious, the way these wretched people keep persecuting him. He's a sensitive, religious person. A darling old man.

## Scene 15

*She smiles radiantly. Flashes go off. The bar: Fred and Joe. Fred still woozy.*

JOE. You think it's true? You think she was mixed up in this lousy business? *(He's pacing, circling, agitated and penned.)*
FRED. Well, yes. Could you stop, possibly, moving, I'm still —
JOE. *(Swallowing Tums.)* Boy that's rotten! And you say you're her friend. What a bastard!
FRED. Hey! Wait a minute! I didn't say she knew what she was doing —

JOE. Yeah, yeah.

FRED. — But carrying messages and whatnot, well, yes, that … happened.

JOE. Takin' it pretty calm, aren't ya? Jesus! She could get ten years! More!

FRED. I'm not calm and I don't imagine she'll really get ten —

JOE. You know those rich friends of hers. Start phoning. Our girl's gonna need fancier shysters than I can afford. *(Joe hands him a phone. Fred holds the phone, paralyzed.)* Whaddya waitin' for?

FRED. I can't think who to call.

JOE. Anybody. Her swanky friends.

FRED. She doesn't have any … *(Cont. to us.)* I called O.J. He was out.

JOE. Go on — try somebody else —

FRED. … I don't know … who — I don't know *who*, Joe.

JOE. Wake up! Think of someone! Popular girl like that — everybody knows her!

FRED. That's the problem.

JOE. What about that geezer thought he was married to her?

FRED. Doc?

JOE. Yeah him —

FRED. Holly'd kill me good if I involved Doc —

JOE. So she kills you good.

FRED. Besides he probably doesn't have any *real* money — not the kind she needs. *(Beat.)*

JOE. *(A command.)* Trawler.

FRED. *That* bastard? Not on your life.

JOE. His money's as green as anybody's. Unless he's pissed on it.

FRED. Exactly.

JOE. *Call him! (Rusty's servant appears.)*

RUSTY'S SERVANT. *Monsieur Trawler pas est ici, malheureusement.*

JOE. *(Grabs phone.)* This is urgent, mister. Life and death.

RUSTY'S SERVANT. *Il est allé pour le mois et n'a pas laissé aucun numéro de téléphone.*

JOE. *Put him on or I'll kill you! (Rusty's servant retreats. Joe and Fred crowd the phone and wait. Mag, grand and Hollywood-matronly, gets on.)*

MAG. Y-y-yes?

FRED. *(To Joe.)* It's Mag. *(To phone.)* Miss Wildwood — Mrs. Trawler, rather — I don't know if you remember me — I'm a friend of Holly Golightly; Fred, she called me, and —

MAG. Are you starkers? My husband and I will positively *sue* anyone who attempts to connect our name to that ro-ro-ro*volt*ing and de-de-*deg*enerate girl. I always *knew* she was a hop-hop-head with no more morals than a hound bitch in heat. Prison is where she belongs. And my husband agrees one thousand percent. We will positively *sue* anyone who — *(Fred hangs up. Lights out on Mag.)*

FRED. *(To us.)* There was nobody else. I just kept calling O.J., over and over again, and downing martinis, and by the time I got him I'd forgotten how to speak. *(O.J. on phone.)*

O.J. Hello? Fred? *(Fred opens his mouth but nothing comes out.)* About the kid, is it? I know already. I spoke already to Iggy Fitelstein. *Iggy's* the best shingle in New York. I said "Iggy you take care of it, send me the bill, only keep my name anonymous, see?" Well, I owe the kid something. Not that I owe her *any*thing, you want to come down to it. She's crazy. A phony. But a *real* phony, you know? Anyway, they only got her on ten thousand bail. Don't worry, Iggy'll spring her tonight — it wouldn't surprise me she's home already.

## Scene 16

*Image: A hospital room. Holly in a hospital bed.*

FRED. *(To us.)* But she wasn't. Nor had she returned the next morning when I went down to feed her cat. Two mornings later, I was sitting by her bedside in a room that reeked of iodine and bed pans, a hospital room. It turned out she'd been there since the night of her arrest.

HOLLY. Well, darling, I lost the baby.

FRED. ... Sorry.

HOLLY. None of that. All for the best, really.

FRED. I brought you Picayunes. You don't look ill — your eyes are clear as rain water and you look all of twelve years.

HOLLY. Good of you to say but — Christ! I nearly cooled. No fooling, the fat woman almost had me. She was yakking up a storm.

FRED. Which fat woman?

HOLLY. Oh. I guess I couldn't have told you about the fat woman. Since I didn't know about her myself until my brother died. Right away, I wondered where he'd gone, what it meant, Fred's dying; and then I saw her, she was there in the room with me, and she had Fred cradled in her arms, a fat, mean-red bitch rocking in a rocking chair with Fred on her lap and laughing like a brass band. Jose, though. Have you … heard any …

FRED. There was this letter waiting, when I went to feed the cat. *(Fred produces the letter. Holly stares at it and her lips form into a tough, aging smile.)*

HOLLY. Darling, would you reach in the drawer there and give me my purse? A girl doesn't read this sort of thing without lipstick. *(She applies maquillage, sprays herself with perfume, puts on earrings, dons dark glasses, then reads. Her smile grows tighter.)* Picayune. *(Fred extracts one, lights it for her; she makes an impatient noise and he applies the cigarette to her mouth.)* Tastes bum. But divine. *(Tosses him letter.)* Maybe this will come in handy — if you ever write a rat-romance. Don't be hoggy: Read it aloud. I'd like to hear it myself.

FRED. *(Reads.)* "My dearest little girl."

HOLLY. What do you think of the handwriting?

FRED. Um — there's nothing to be thought — tight — legible —

HOLLY. It's him to a T. Buttoned up and constipated. Go on.

FRED. "My dearest little girl, I have loved you knowing you were not as others. But conceive of my despair upon discovering in such a brutal and public style how very different you are from the manner of woman a man of my faith and career could hope to make his wife. Verily I grief for the disgrace of your present circumstance, and do not find it in my heart to add my condemn to the condemn that surrounds you. So I hope you will find it in your heart not to condemn me. I have my family to protect, and my name, and I am a coward where these institutions enter. Forget me, beautiful child. I am no longer here. I am gone home. But may God always be with you and your child. May God not be the same as — Jose."

HOLLY. All right, he's not a rat without reason. A super-sized King Kong-type rat like Rusty. Benny Shacklett. But oh gee, golly goddamn, I *did* love him. The rat.

FRED. Holly, we have to make plans.

HOLLY. Oh plans.

FRED. This isn't a joke.

HOLLY. You're too young to be so stuffy. And, what business is it of yours, anyway?

FRED. I'm your friend. And I'm worried. What do you intend doing?

HOLLY. Today's Wednesday, isn't it? So I suppose I'll sleep until Saturday, really get a good schluffen. Saturday morning I'll skip out to the bank. Then I'll stop by the apartment and pick up a night-gown or two and my Mainbocher. Following which, I'll report to Idlewild. Where, as you damn well know, I have a perfectly fine reservation on a perfectly fine plane. And since you're such a friend I'll let you wave me off. *Please* stop shaking your head.

FRED. Just what kind of pills have they been feeding you here? Can't you realize you're under a criminal indictment? If they catch you jumping bail, they'll throw away the key. Even if you get away with it, you'll never be able to come home.

HOLLY. Home is where you feel at home. I'm still looking.

FRED. No, Holly, it's stupid. You're innocent. You've got to stick it out.

HOLLY. Rah, team, rah. *(She blows smoke in his face.)* Oh screw it. *(Stabs out cigarette.)* I have a fair chance they won't catch me. Provided you keep your *bouche fermez.* Look. Don't despise me, darling. I haven't much choice. I talked it over with the lawyer: All the badgers want from me is my services as a state's witness against Sally. Well, I may be rotten to the core, Maude, *but:* testify against a friend I will not. Anyway, this town's dead for me. Certain shades of limelight wreck a girl's complexion. Do me a favor, darling. Call up the *Times* or whatever you call, and get a list of the fifty richest men in Brazil. I'm *not* kidding. The fifty richest — regardless of race or color. And poke around my apartment until you find that medal you gave me. The St. Christopher. I'll need it for the trip. *(Rain starts.)*

FRED. *(To us.)* It was utter folly. There was nothing for it but to submit.

# Scene 17

*Outside the brownstone.*

JOE. Fred! She's going from the hospital to the bank then straight to the bar. She wants you to pack her stuff. Her jewelry. Her guitar. Tooth brushes and things. And a bottle of hundred-year-old brandy:

She says you'll find it down in the bottom of the dirty-clothes basket. Yeah, oh, and the cat. She wants the cat. But hell, I don't know we should help her at all. She ought to be protected against herself. Me, I feel like telling the cops. Maybe if I go back and build her some drinks, maybe I can get her drunk enough to call it off.

FRED. What plane is going to take off in this monsoon, anyway?

JOE. You're right. *(Beat.)* You got a half-hour. *(Torrential rain blotting everything. Next we see it's the bar. There are flowers in a vase. Holly and Joe Bell are there:)*

## Scene 18

HOLLY. You're late, buster. Did you bring the brandy?

FRED. Here. *(He presents it to her. The cat makes an appearance here too, somehow.)*

HOLLY. This was meant to be part of my hope chest. The idea was, every anniversary we'd have a swig. Thank Jesus I never bought the chest. Mr. Bell, sir, three glasses.

JOE. You'll only need two. I won't drink to your foolishness.

HOLLY. Ah, Mr. Bell. The lady doesn't vanish every day. Won't you toast her?

JOE. I'll have no part of it. If you're going to hell, you'll go on your own. With no further help from me.

HOLLY. *(Re: something outside.)* What's that? *(Possibly an image of a limousine appears.)*

JOE. It's nothing. One of them Carey Cadillacs. I hired it. To take you to the airport.

HOLLY. Kind, dear Mr. Bell. Look at me, sir. *(He doesn't. He takes flowers from their vase and thrusts them at her but misses and they scatter.)*

JOE. Goodbye. *(Looking about to vomit, he runs off, presumably to the men's room.)*

# Scene 19

*Into the car. The staging of this possibly a projection of them entering, then their standing in attitudes of passengers: Holly, Fred, the cat. Lights and images and sound giving us the ride. They don't talk, but Holly seems to be searching for something in what passes out the window.*

FRED. *(To us.)* We rode in dreadful silence, thankful for the noise the rain made.

HOLLY. Stop here. *(Sound of car lurching to a halt.)*

FRED. What are you doing? Why are we stopping?

HOLLY. Last bit of business to take care of. *(Holly gets out of car with cat.)* What do you think? This ought to be the right kind of place for a tough guy like you. Garbage cans. Rats galore. Plenty of cat-bums to gang around with. So scram. *(She puts down cat.)* Beat it. *(Cat runs away. She returns to car.)* Go. Go. Go.

FRED. Well, you *are*. You *are* a bitch.

HOLLY. I told you. We just met by the river one day: That's all. Independents, both of us. We never made each other any promises. We never — *(Something happens to her. She bolts from the car, runs. Fred follows.)* You. Cat. Where are you? Here, cat.

FRED. Cat! Cat! *(Nothing. Holly collapses into Fred's arms.)*

HOLLY. Oh, Jesus God. We did belong to each other. He was mine.

FRED. I'll find him. *(She looks at him entreatingly.)* I'll take care of him, too. I promise.

HOLLY. But what about me? I'm very scared, buster. Yes, at last. Because it could go on forever. Not knowing what's yours until you've thrown it away. The mean reds, they're nothing — the fat woman — This, though: My mouth's so dry, if my life depended on it I couldn't spit. *(She goes back into the car, Fred follows.)* Sorry. Let's go.

## Scene 20

*1957. Faintly, these headlines in the background, in succession: "Tomato's Tomato Missing," "Drug-Case Actress Believed Gangland Victim," "Fleeing Playgirl Traced to Rio."*

FRED. Apparently, no attempt was made by American authorities to recover her, and soon the matter diminished to an occasional gossip-column mention. As a news story, it was revived only once: on Christmas Day, when Sally Tomato died of a heart attack in Sing Sing. Months went by, a winter of them, and not a word from Holly. But in the spring a postcard came. It was scribbled in pencil and signed with a lipstick kiss. *(Holly appears.)*

HOLLY. Darling. Brazil was beastly but Buenos Aires the best. Not Tiffany's but almost. Am joined at the hip with duh*vine* señor. Love? Think so. Anyhoo am looking for somewhere to live (Señor has wife, seven brats) and will let you know address when I know it myself. *Mille tendresse. (She remains, looking hopeful.)*

FRED. But the address, if it ever existed, was never sent, which made me sad, there was so much I wanted to write her. That I'd sold *two* stories, had read where the Trawlers were counter-suing for divorce, was moving out of the brownstone because it was haunted. But mostly, I wanted to tell her about the cat. I had kept my promise; I found him. It took weeks of after-work roaming through those Spanish Harlem streets, and there were many false alarms — flashes of tiger-striped fur that, upon inspection, were not him. But one day, one cold, sunshiny Sunday winter afternoon, it was. *(Image of apartment building window, black and white with the cat in color.)* Flanked by potted plants and framed by clean lace curtains, he was seated in the window of a warm-looking room: I wondered what his name was, for I was certain he had one now, certain he'd arrived somewhere he belonged. African hut or whatever, I hope Holly has too.

## End of Play

# PROPERTY LIST

Bar accoutrement: liquor bottles, glasses, ice, etc.
Photographs in a manila envelope
Roller skates
Glass of brandy
Georges Simenon novel
Bowl of fruit with an apple
Alarm clock
Gift basket with handwritten card
Guitar
Piece of paper, pen
Book with newspaper clippings stashed inside
Cat
Bottle of scotch
Large envelope
Cheap masks
Large decorative birdcage
St. Christopher medallion
Sun lamp
Suntan oil
Hamburg Heaven sign
Hamburger meal
Wallet with snapshots inside
Tabloid newspaper
Telegram
Hypodermic needle
Cooking utensils
Knitting in progress
Liniment
Telephone
Letter
Makeup in purse
Dark glasses
Picayune cigarettes, matches
Flowers in vase
Bottle of old, good brandy

# SOUND EFFECTS

Rainstorm
Background hum of people at a party
Loud party
Learn-Portuguese record playing
Record needle scratch
Beautiful day in Central Park
Sound of children taunting in English and Spanish
Rocks being thrown
Traffic swerving away
People panicking, cheering
Police siren
Typing
Press flash bulbs going off
Car ride in the rain

# NEW PLAYS

★ **AGES OF THE MOON by Sam Shepard.** Byron and Ames are old friends, reunited by mutual desperation. Over bourbon on ice, they sit, reflect and bicker until fifty years of love, friendship and rivalry are put to the test at the barrel of a gun. "A poignant and honest continuation of themes that have always been present in the work of one of this country's most important dramatists, here reconsidered in the light and shadow of time passed." –NY Times. "Finely wrought…as enjoyable and enlightening as a night spent stargazing." –Talkin' Broadway. [2M] ISBN: 978-0-8222-2462-4

★ **ALL THE WAY by Robert Schenkkan. Winner of the 2014 Tony Award for Best Play.** November, 1963. An assassin's bullet catapults Lyndon Baines Johnson into the presidency. A Shakespearean figure of towering ambition and appetite, this charismatic, conflicted Texan hurls himself into the passage of the Civil Rights Act—a tinderbox issue emblematic of a divided America—even as he campaigns for re-election in his own right, and the recognition he so desperately wants. In Pulitzer Prize and Tony Award–winning Robert Schenkkan's vivid dramatization of LBJ's first year in office, means versus ends plays out on the precipice of modern America. ALL THE WAY is a searing, enthralling exploration of the morality of power. It's not personal, it's just politics. "…action-packed, thoroughly gripping… jaw-dropping political drama." –Variety. "A theatrical coup…nonstop action. The suspense of a first-class thriller." –NY1. [17M, 3W] ISBN: 978-0-8222-3181-3

★ **CHOIR BOY by Tarell Alvin McCraney.** The Charles R. Drew Prep School for Boys is dedicated to the creation of strong, ethical black men. Pharus wants nothing more than to take his rightful place as leader of the school's legendary gospel choir. Can he find his way inside the hallowed halls of this institution if he sings in his own key? "[An] affecting and honest portrait…of a gay youth tentatively beginning to find the courage to let the truth about himself become known." –NY Times. "In his stirring and stylishly told drama, Tarell Alvin McCraney cannily explores race and sexuality and the graces and gravity of history." –NY Daily News. [7M] ISBN: 978-0-8222-3116-5

★ **THE ELECTRIC BABY by Stefanie Zadravec.** When Helen causes a car accident that kills a young man, a group of fractured souls cross paths and connect around a mysterious dying baby who glows like the moon. Folk tales and folklore weave throughout this magical story of sad endings, strange beginnings and the unlikely people that get you from one place to the next. "The imperceptible magic that pervades human existence and the power of myth to assuage sorrow are invoked by the playwright as she entwines the lives of strangers in THE ELECTRIC BABY, a touching drama." –NY Times. "As dazzling as the dialogue is dreamful." –Pittsburgh City Paper. [3M, 3W] ISBN: 978-0-8222-3011-3

**DRAMATISTS PLAY SERVICE, INC.**
**440 Park Avenue South, New York, NY 10016  212-683-8960  Fax 212-213-1539**
postmaster@dramatists.com  www.dramatists.com

# NEW PLAYS

★ **I'LL EAT YOU LAST: A CHAT WITH SUE MENGERS by John Logan.** For more than 20 years, Sue Mengers' clients were the biggest names in show business: Barbra Streisand, Faye Dunaway, Burt Reynolds, Ali MacGraw, Gene Hackman, Cher, Candice Bergen, Ryan O'Neal, Nick Nolte, Mike Nichols, Gore Vidal, Bob Fosse…If her clients were the talk of the town, she was the town, and her dinner parties were the envy of Hollywood. Now, you're invited into her glamorous Beverly Hills home for an evening of dish, dirty secrets and all the inside showbiz details only Sue can tell you. "A delectable soufflé of a solo show…thanks to the buoyant, witty writing of Mr. Logan" –NY Times. "80 irresistible minutes of primo tinseltown dish from a certified master chef." –Hollywood Reporter. [1W] ISBN: 978-0-8222-3079-3

★ **PUNK ROCK by Simon Stephens.** In a private school outside of Manchester, England, a group of highly-articulate seventeen-year-olds flirt and posture their way through the day while preparing for their A-Level mock exams. With hormones raging and minimal adult supervision, the students must prepare for their future — and survive the savagery of high school. Inspired by playwright Simon Stephens' own experiences as a teacher, PUNK ROCK is an honest and unnerving chronicle of contemporary adolescence. "[A] tender, ferocious and frightning play." –NY Times. "[A] muscular little play that starts out funny and ferocious then reveals its compassion by degrees." –Hollywood Reporter. [5M, 3W] ISBN: 978-0-8222-3288-9

★ **THE COUNTRY HOUSE by Donald Margulies.** A brood of famous and longing-to-be-famous creative artists have gathered at their summer home during the Williamstown Theatre Festival. When the weekend takes an unexpected turn, everyone is forced to improvise, inciting a series of simmering jealousies, romantic outbursts, and passionate soul-searching. Both witty and compelling, THE COUNTRY HOUSE provides a piercing look at a family of performers coming to terms with the roles they play in each other's lives. "A valentine to the artists of the stage." –NY Times. "Remarkably candid and funny." –Variety. [3M, 3W] ISBN: 978-0-8222-3274-2

★ **OUR LADY OF KIBEHO by Katori Hall.** Based on real events, OUR LADY OF KIBEHO is an exploration of faith, doubt, and the power and consequences of both. In 1981, a village girl in Rwanda claims to see the Virgin Mary. Ostracized by her schoolmates and labeled disturbed, everyone refuses to believe, until impossible happenings appear again and again. Skepticism gives way to fear, and then to belief, causing upheaval in the school community and beyond. "Transfixing." –NY Times. "Hall's passionate play renews belief in what theater can do." –Time Out [7M, 8W, 1 boy] ISBN: 978-0-8222-3301-5

**DRAMATISTS PLAY SERVICE, INC.**
440 Park Avenue South, New York, NY 10016 212-683-8960 Fax 212-213-1539
postmaster@dramatists.com www.dramatists.com

# NEW PLAYS

★ **ACT ONE by James Lapine.** Growing up in an impoverished Bronx family and forced to drop out of school at age thirteen, Moss Hart dreamed of joining the glamorous world of the theater. Hart's famous memoir *Act One* plots his unlikely collaboration with the legendary playwright George S. Kaufman and his arrival on Broadway. Tony Award-winning writer and director James Lapine has adapted Act One for the stage, creating a funny, heartbreaking and suspenseful celebration of a playwright and his work. "...brims contagiously with the ineffable, irrational and irrefutable passion for that endangered religion called the Theater." –NY Times. "...wrought with abundant skill and empathy." –Time Out. [8M, 4W] ISBN: 978-0-8222-3217-9

★ **THE VEIL by Conor McPherson.** May 1822, rural Ireland. The defrocked Reverend Berkeley arrives at the crumbling former glory of Mount Prospect House to accompany a young woman to England. Seventeen-year-old Hannah is to be married off to a marquis in order to resolve the debts of her mother's estate. However, compelled by the strange voices that haunt his beautiful young charge and a fascination with the psychic current that pervades the house, Berkeley proposes a séance, the consequences of which are catastrophic. "...an effective mixture of dark comedy and suspense." –Telegraph (London). "A cracking fireside tale of haunting and decay." –Times (London). [3M, 5W] ISBN: 978-0-8222-3313-8

★ **AN OCTOROON by Branden Jacobs-Jenkins. Winner of the 2014 OBIE Award for Best New American Play.** Judge Peyton is dead and his plantation Terrebonne is in financial ruins. Peyton's handsome nephew George arrives as heir apparent and quickly falls in love with Zoe, a beautiful octoroon. But the evil overseer M'Closky has other plans—for both Terrebonne and Zoe. In 1859, a famous Irishman wrote this play about slavery in America. Now an American tries to write his own. "AN OCTOROON invites us to laugh loudly and easily at how naïve the old stereotypes now seem, until nothing seems funny at all." –NY Times [10M, 5W] ISBN: 978-0-8222-3226-1

★ **IVANOV translated and adapted by Curt Columbus.** In this fascinating early work by Anton Chekhov, we see the union of humor and pathos that would become his trademark. A restless man, Nicholai Ivanov struggles to dig himself out of debt and out of provincial boredom. When the local doctor, Lvov, informs Ivanov that his wife Anna is dying and accuses him of worsening her condition with his foul moods, Ivanov is sent into a downward spiral of depression and ennui. He soon finds himself drawn to a beautiful young woman, Sasha, full of hope and energy. Finding himself stuck between a romantic young mistress and his ailing wife, Ivanov falls deeper into crisis, heading toward inevitable tragedy. [8M, 8W] ISBN: 978-0-8222-3155-4

**DRAMATISTS PLAY SERVICE, INC.**
**440 Park Avenue South, New York, NY 10016  212-683-8960  Fax 212-213-1539**
**postmaster@dramatists.com  www.dramatists.com**

# NEW PLAYS

★ **MOTHERS AND SONS by Terrence McNally.** At turns funny and powerful, MOTHERS AND SONS portrays a woman who pays an unexpected visit to the New York apartment of her late son's partner, who is now married to another man and has a young son. Challenged to face how society has changed around her, generations collide as she revisits the past and begins to see the life her son might have led. "A resonant elegy for a ravaged generation." –NY Times. "A moving reflection on a changed America." –Chicago Tribune. [2M, 1W, 1 boy] ISBN: 978-0-8222-3183-7

★ **THE HEIR APPARENT by David Ives, adapted from Le Légataire Universel by Jean-François Regnard.** Paris, 1708. Eraste, a worthy though penniless young man, is in love with the fair Isabelle, but her forbidding mother, Madame Argante, will only let the two marry if Eraste can show he will inherit the estate of his rich but miserly Uncle Geronte. Unfortunately, old Geronte has also fallen for the fair Isabelle, and plans to marry her this very day and leave her everything in his will—separating the two young lovers forever. Eraste's wily servant Crispin jumps in, getting a couple of meddling relatives disinherited by impersonating them (one, a brash American, the other a French female country cousin)—only to have the old man kick off before his will is made! In a brilliant stroke, Crispin then impersonates the old man, dictating a will favorable to his master (and Crispin himself, of course)—only to find that rich Uncle Geronte isn't dead at all and is more than ever ready to marry Isabelle! The multiple strands of the plot are unraveled to great comic effect in the streaming rhyming couplets of French classical comedy, and everyone lives happily, and richly, ever after. [4M, 3W] ISBN: 978-0-8222-2808-0

★ **HANDLE WITH CARE by Jason Odell Williams.** Circumstances both hilarious and tragic bring together a young Israeli woman, who has little command of English, and a young American man, who has little command of romance. Is their inevitable love an accident…or is it destiny, generations in the making? "A hilarious and heartwarming romantic comedy." –NY Times. "Hilariously funny! Utterly charming, fearlessly adorable and a tiny bit magical." –Naples News. [2M, 2W] ISBN: 978-0-8222-3138-7

★ **LAST GAS by John Cariani.** Nat Paradis is a Red Sox-loving part-time dad who manages Paradis' Last Convenient Store, the last convenient place to get gas—or anything—before the Canadian border to the north and the North Maine Woods to the west. When an old flame returns to town, Nat gets a chance to rekindle a romance he gave up on years ago. But sparks fly as he's forced to choose between new love and old. "Peppered with poignant characters [and] sharp writing." –Portland Phoenix. "Very funny and surprisingly thought-provoking." –Portland Press Herald. [4M, 3W] ISBN: 978-0-8222-3232-2

**DRAMATISTS PLAY SERVICE, INC.**
**440 Park Avenue South, New York, NY 10016  212-683-8960  Fax 212-213-1539**
postmaster@dramatists.com  www.dramatists.com